Toward a Right Relationship with Finance:
Debt, Interest, Growth, and Security

D1518951

QIF Focus Books

Toward a Right Relationship with Finance:
Debt, Interest, Growth, and Security

Pamela Haines, Ed Dreby

David Kane, Charles Blanchard

QIF Focus Book 9
Quaker Institute for the Future 2016

Published for Quaker Institute for the Future by *Producciones de la Hamaca*, Caye Caulker, Belize <producciones-hamaca.com> ISBN: 978-976-8142-88-7 (paperback) and ISBN: 978-976-8142-89-4 (e-book)

Toward a Right Relationship with Finance: Debt, Interest, Growth, and Security is the ninth in the series of *QIF Focus Books* ISBN: 978-976-8142-90-0 (formerly *Quaker Institute for the Future Pamphlets*)

This book was printed on-demand by Lightning Source, Inc (LSI). The on-demand printing system is environmentally friendly because books are printed as needed, instead of in large numbers that might end up in someone's basement or a dump site. In addition, LSI is committed to using materials obtained by sustainable forestry practices. LSI is certified by Sustainable Forestry Initiative (SFI® Certificate Number: PwC-SFICOC-345 SFI-00980). The Sustainable Forestry Initiative is an independent, internationally recognized non-profit organization responsible for the SFI certification standard, the world's largest single forest certification standard. The SFI program is based on the premise that responsible environmental behavior and sound business decisions can co-exist to the benefit of communities, customers and the environment, today and for future generations <sfiprogram.org>.

QIF Focus Books aim to provide critical information and understanding born of careful discernment on social, economic, and ecological realities, inspired by the testimonies and values of the Religious Society of Friends (Quakers). We live in a time when social and ecological issues are converging toward catastrophic breakdown. Human adaptation to social, economic and planetary realities must be re-thought and re-designed. *QIF Focus Books* are dedicated to this calling based on a spiritual and ethical commitment to "right relationship" with Earth's whole commonwealth of life.   <quakerinstitute.org>

Producciones de la Hamaca is dedicated to:

—Celebration and documentation of Earth and all her inhabitants,
—Restoration and conservation of Earth's natural resources,
—Creative expression of the sacredness of Earth and Spirit.

Contents

Acknowledgments

The authors gratefully thank Marianne Comfort, Leonard Joy, and John Lodenkamper, who read drafts with care, flagged problematic sections, and helped shape the text. As the editor and publisher, Judy Lumb polished the final book.

We were greatly aided by those who contributed text and sidebars. Deb Foote Faulkner and Hollister Knowlton, along with Dave Kane, Ed Dreby, and Pamela Haines, added personal dimensions with their sidebars.

The authors are particularly indebted to Leonard Joy for his contributions, some of which appear in a sidebar and some of which have been woven throughout the book, especially in Chapter 4.

We thank the author and publisher for permission to reprint excerpts from "Epilogue: Down to Earth with an Eye on the Future," the concluding chapter of Keith Helmuth's book, *Tracking Down Ecological Guidance: Presence, Beauty, Survival*.

Chapters 3, 4, and 5 build upon the fifth and sixth *QIF Focus Books*: *It's the Economy, Friend: Understanding the Growth Dilemma* and *Beyond the Growth Dilemma: Toward an Ecologically Integrated Economy*.[1] The authors appreciate the opportunity to extend this prior work.

Preface

The regional association of Quakers in Pennsylvania had gone through some very lean and painful years following the 2008 Great Recession. It took several years to take stock of the depth of our financial difficulties, followed by painful adjustments including laying off over a third of our paid staff and slashing program expenses to the bone, and several more years of tight fiscal controls, forced savings and austerity spending. Finally, at our annual business sessions in the summer of 2014, Philadelphia Yearly Meeting heard the news we had been longing to hear. Spending was stable; resources were up; income was showing a tendency to rise. If the stock market would just continue to grow, we could anticipate more reassuring financial statements for years to come.

"If the stock market would just continue to grow…" That phrase rang in the ears of several of us who were active in our community's Friends Economic Integrity Project. One of us articulated this concern to the larger body. "It is a paradox," he said. "We wish for growth in the stock market. Yet that growth inevitably brings growth in economic inequality." Others in the group would have added that Wall Street growth also brings growth in environmental destruction.

Several of us gathered at the end of these sessions to consider ways forward. We had a shared critique of the role of financial speculation in an economy addicted to growth, which is increasingly inequitable and ecologically unsustainable. But with institutional endowments so deeply dependent on these investments, and with many people now counting as never before on the performance of Wall Street for our retirement security, how could we challenge this system with integrity and effectiveness? It seemed that individuals in our society would have to break with our dependence on financial speculation for our retirement security before we could gather the necessary will to make a transformative change.

We knew very little about how this could be done. But we knew the outlines of the challenge, and some of the important questions to ask. As we began talking with colleagues in the Economic Integrity Project and other Friends, the goals of this book began to take clearer shape:

- to help others understand how our current economic system is based on unearned income on the one hand, and debt on the other, with a built-in momentum toward economic inequality and ecological overshoot;

- to frame the conversation within the context of our deepest values and beliefs;

- to suggest plausible and historically grounded alternatives to the current system, particularly with regard to financing retirement;

- and to invite everyone both to imagine new and more durable kinds of security and to take action on behalf of the future.

Much good work has been done to shed light on the history of economic thought, the realities of our current economic situation, and the impacts on wealth distribution, social welfare and environmental threats. There is also much good thinking, many exciting models, and new developments across the globe around building a new economy. Addressing all these topics is clearly beyond the scope of this endeavor. The purpose of this project is to help gain clarity about the ways that so many of us are personally entangled with our financial system, particularly around debt and income from savings related to retirement planning.

This book is addressed to those of us who find ourselves faced with difficult financial dilemmas for living our testimonies in what has been described as a "now but not yet world." It includes understanding the history and roots of that entanglement, considering what alternatives might be possible, and suggesting possible steps that might be taken to act with greater power and integrity — both on a personal level and in service to change on a larger level.

Chapter 1 introduces our motivating concerns, provides a framework for considering those concerns, and identifies some of the current dilemmas we face.

Chapter 2 provides a consideration of ethics and values in borrowing and lending, including a historical overview of societal attitudes and practices around debt and usury.

Chapter 3 describes the role of savings and debt in a very basic summary of how, in theory, market economies are supposed to function. Chapter 4 looks at how our economic system has shifted its ethical focus during the past 75 years from serving the common good to favoring private gain, with rather obvious success for a few and a troubling future for society as a whole. Chapter 5 briefly summarizes recent understanding of environmental limits to economic growth.

These beginning chapters lead to a consideration of how our society's current realities complicate the challenge of managing household finances in a realistic and ethically responsible way. We'll examine the roots of our entanglement with investments for retirement, institutional endowments, and college costs in Chapter 6, and consider investment alternatives in Chapter 7.

What does this portend for creating a future economic system that provides greater economic security for the lives of ordinary people? We look at our society's history of providing for the common good, and consider some of the options for doing this more adequately in Chapter 8. In view of concerns about public sector finances and government debt, where would the resources for providing greater economic security come from? We suggest some ideas in Chapter 9.

What might general welfare and retirement security look like in the future? What are steps we can take as individuals and as citizens to move ourselves and our society in a direction that has a future? We will close with an exploration of these possibilities in Chapter 10.

Pamela Haines, Ed Dreby
David Kane, and Charles Blanchard
January, 2016

CHAPTER 1
Introduction

Many of us are worried. Somehow, amidst all of the wealth of our country, our security is slipping away. The business headline: "the Dow Jones has surged back and reached new levels," may seem like good news, but it does not bring a deep sense of well-being. We find ourselves scrambling to pay our bills, get out of debt, help our children get out of debt, and save up for retirement that seems far from certain.

As a result, with so much of so many people's focus on trying to prop up our own individual security, we are having a harder and harder time thinking about the security of the whole. We know it is threatened. We watch our economic system working less and less well for more and more people. Wealth is concentrating at the top. Big chunks of the middle class are slipping downhill, and the numbers of poor are growing. The burst of the housing bubble wiped out the only assets of many people, hitting particularly hard working people for whom home owning has been a major form of asset accumulation.

We can't help but worry about loved ones who come after us, the enormous threats to their security, and the security of life on this planet. We watch the threats to our environment — and the whole commonwealth of life — mounting, while our economic and political systems seem caught in a trajectory that increases these threats rather than addressing them.

Something is badly askew, and it's not surprising that we are worried and bewildered. It's hard enough to try to understand what's going on, let alone try to make anything better. Just trying to keep afloat ourselves, help our loved ones have a decent life, and do our best to be responsible in facing our own old age feels like more than enough to handle.

Yet, our world is crying out for thoughtful people to engage our best thinking and deepest values with this system. We may not know the answers. The levers of power may seem hopelessly far away. Yet one of the obstacles to engaging our best thinking and deepest values is our own entanglement with the financial system that is a driver of many of these problems. If we are dependent on the stock market for our future security, how can we question the seeming imperative for its growth? If all our attention goes to individual solutions to individual indebtedness, how can we see the larger picture?

However, as we find ways to act with greater integrity in our own financial affairs, we find more solid ground on which to stand, larger vistas of possibilities, and encouragement to take additional steps. But the goal of individual financial security is a mirage. We're all in this boat together. As we improve the relationships between our personal finances and our values, we put ourselves in a stronger position to help advance our shared financial security.

A Context of Values

We can only try to do the right thing while living in a system that currently functions in ways incompatible with many of our values. As we have conversations about how our faith and values apply to our own decisions about borrowing, saving, and investing, we will be shining a light on larger issues. As we share our personal discernment about acting with greater integrity in our finances, we will be drawing others into the conversation. As we are moved to take broader actions as a consequence of this process, we will be part of a larger process of change, calling for a realignment of our financial world that would conform more closely to our ethical and faith traditions.

Values and faith belong in this conversation. Many economists claim that they have made their discipline a values-free, objective, and mathematically based science.

2

In the process, they have distorted it by including in their calculations only that which is easily measurable, like money flow. They have defined human behavior solely on the basis of our relationship to money; excluded motivations of love, generosity, and service to the whole; and ignored impacts on the social fabric that are not strictly monetary.

Yet, economic systems are built on deeply value-laden assumptions. Consider very basic questions like the following: What is wealth? What has value? What increases well-being? When is "more" better than "less?" What motivates people? Do we have a responsibility to the future? Adam Smith, generally considered the father of economics, is best known for his metaphor of the "invisible hand" by which the private self-interested choices of individuals, mediated through a free market, will generate results that are good for all. But in *Wealth of Nations* he discusses economics in explicitly moral terms, where markets both depend upon and produce not only prosperity but also justice and freedom, particularly for the poor. He saw capitalism as an ethical project, the success of which required political commitment to these values.[2] When we think more specifically about the financial systems with which we interact, the questions become more specific as well, but no less values based. They become intensely relevant for people of faith:

- Should people who have not yet started working be in debt?
- Should it be easier for people with some assets to get more than for people with no assets to get some?
- If there is "no time but this present" why are we laying away treasures for the future?
- Does having something mean we have a right to it?
- Do we have a right to income that we haven't earned by our own time and effort?
- What if my gain in economic security involves someone else's loss?
- What does inequality do to our sense of connection?

3

- When does debt become indebtedness?
- Should the economy serve the common good?
- Should our goal be individual or collective security?

People of faith have grappled with these issues for as long as faith has been around. Over the centuries faith traditions have reproached the conduct and condemned the systems that consign whole sectors of the population to misery. Old Testament law prescribed periodic jubilee years when all debts were to be forgiven. For a thousand years the Christian church kept strong prohibitions against charging interest on borrowed money, as Islam still does. In the eighteenth and nineteenth centuries, courageous religious leaders addressed the human fall-out of debt servitude and the industrial revolution; in the late twentieth, they called for debt forgiveness for heavily burdened third world countries. We have strong shoulders on which to stand.

Current Dilemmas

We need all the strength we can get. We are faced with challenges on all fronts. At the personal level, debt has risen exponentially in recent decades. The bursting of the housing bubble has left millions with underwater housing mortgages. Tens of millions of people are now burdened with tens of thousands of dollars in student debt. Many more have credit card debt, with interest rates that would be categorized by the old Christian church as usurious. Those who don't have access to credit are increasingly turning to the new industry of payday lending, where interest rates are even higher.

Only the most fortunate among us are facing retirement with equanimity. Those with some assets anxiously squirrel away money, with one eye on current bills and another on the stock market, in constant unease that we're making the wrong choices or it won't be enough. Those who are counting on pensions worry about how underfunded they are. And those with none of these assets face the prospects of living off meager Social Security benefits.

Our institutional assets are at risk as well. How many of our meetings and churches, schools and non-profit organizations

4

have struggled with painful issues of downsizing staff, deferred maintenance and cutting back services as the value of endowments shrank, assets disappeared, and the financial capacity of their members diminished? And what does it do to a faith community to have its security dependent on financial markets?

The state of our societal economic well-being in general is too broad a topic for this book, and is addressed in depth in many other places. But it is deeply troubling on many fronts. As people of faith, we value equality, yet we see economic inequality increasing dramatically, with racial minorities experiencing the brunt of both income inequality and environmental damage. We value integrity, yet the Gross Domestic Product is a false measure of prosperity, and truth is being sacrificed in advertising, mass media, public discourse and politics. We value simplicity, yet our growth economy requires ever-increasing consumption, debt, and intrusion on the natural world to sustain itself. We value community. Yet, we are deeply divided by racism; the numbers of those facing economic insecurity and confined to prisons continue to increase; and God's community of life is diminished. We value peace, yet the violence and devastation caused by our economic system's exploitation of both people and planet is alarming.

On a planetary scale, we are facing a profound dilemma. As our economies currently operate, they require growth to function. People with plenty are induced to acquire more and those in debt are induced to borrow more. Yet more growth makes the wealthiest even wealthier, while unemployment, hunger and violence are widespread. And human economies are already far larger than Earth's commonwealth of life can continue to support.

Is there a connection between debt and the growth imperative of our current economic system? In our current system, as explained in Chapter 3, virtually all money is created when banks make loans. And, when banks charge interest on loans, they inevitably create more debt than they add to the money supply.

This generates an endless demand to make more money in order to pay off more debt. Since making more money leads to using more resources, Earth's ecological systems are increasingly strained. This perspective is not within the mainstream of economic awareness, but it gives pause to people who consider the drivers of environmental destruction and their relationship to a growth-driven economy.

While these questions are not new, they have become matters of great urgency for those who are attuned to the realities of systemic economic injustice and ecological destruction. Our current system seems less and less capable of providing for the public welfare, and much of the wealth in the country is not serving the common good. As the dynamics of our current system increasingly press against the limits of our planet, it is critical that we engage in thoughtful debate about the kinds of economic policies that allow us a future.

Looking Forward

It's hard to think clearly about a system with which we are thoroughly entangled. From a personal perspective, borrowing involves spending money one doesn't possess, and saving involves not spending money one does possess. But from a systemic perspective, borrowing and lending are two sides of the same coin, both of which are affected by what has become the standard practice of charging interest on borrowed money.

Those of us who are experiencing hardship may feel ashamed of struggling with debt, seeing it as a personal failing. Feeling isolated and inadequate, we may not speak up. Those of us who are trying to manage savings in an ethically sensitive way may feel uncertain about how best to do it, and uneasy about having opportunities that seem unavailable to others. Feeling separated and insecure, we may not speak out. This entanglement and dependency constrains our imagination and saps our ability to consider and actively work toward alternatives.

As we face the implications of continuing in the same direction, we are challenged to imagine new possibilities. We need to develop some very different ways of organizing our economy, and an exit strategy from the current one. The first requires an enormous exercise of the imagination, and lots of experimentation with different forms on a local scale. The second requires both an understanding of the systems that will need to be redesigned and a withdrawal of our loyalties from the old system.

It always helps to start with a vision. Here are a few possible elements. **For ourselves:**

- Our yearning to learn and serve in the present is not constrained by fear of destitution.
- We need no more than modest savings; basic education, health and old age needs can be assured.
- None of us enters adulthood in debt.
- Our excess money, or time that would have been spent earning extra income, can be devoted to serving the community, and the commonwealth of life.

For society at large:

- The main purpose of the economy will be to provide livelihoods for all, rather than wealth for a few.
- All members of society will be treated with dignity; no groups will serve as scapegoats, distracting us from the failure of our societal institutions.
- Freely elected governments will have the power to establish measures of common well-being, and require institutions to serve the common good.
- Earth's resources will be used more sparingly as advertising and consumption lose their grip.
- Systems of finance will support the general welfare.
- As we face the threats of climate change and environmental destruction, our economic institutions and policies will be part of the solution rather than part of the problem.

This is not beyond the realm of possibility. In 1944, Franklin Roosevelt spoke in his inaugural address of an economic bill of rights. "Necessitous men are not free men," he said. Since "true individual freedom cannot exist without economic security and independence," the original Bill of Rights must be supplemented by eight rights that "spell security." The proposed rights include the right to a useful and remunerative job, adequate medical care, education, and protection from the economic fears of old age, sickness, accident, and unemployment.[3]

Governmental tax, regulation and subsidy policies in the 1950s and 1960s created and defended an expanding middle class. While we had not arrived at FDR's economic bill of rights, we were headed in that direction. Massive changes in the economic and political landscape since the 1970s have brought us to our current situation, and massive changes are needed again on both fronts to shift our course back toward an expanding middle class and decreasing income inequality.

CHAPTER 2
Ethics and Values
in Borrowing and Lending

The practice of lending money at interest did not become an accepted part of economic life in western societies until fairly recent times. Nor is it practiced everywhere throughout the world today. Here we examine historical developments leading to contemporary western practices of borrowing and lending, and social and religious attitudes toward debt, interest, and the accumulation of wealth. With this historical perspective, it becomes easier to see that the contemporary economic system in which we are living is but one way to organize exchanges of goods and services. Different sets of economic relationships have been, and still are, practiced among people in other societies. Before considering these larger historical, social and philosophical views, some comments and questions about borrowing and lending in our personal lives may help ground us in our own values and ethics.

Being in someone's debt can be seen positively, as something that connects us to each other. When I am in your debt, you have provided me with something of value, which arouses in me a natural desire to reciprocate. This falls within the human tradition of giving and receiving gifts. But when a desire to reciprocate shifts to an obligation to reciprocate, we arrive at the more common and potentially problematic understanding of debt.

When you have given me something of value, do I feel an obligation to return something of value? Should this be of equal or greater value? Of a similar kind of value? If I give you something of value, do I assume that you have an obligation to give something back to me? If so, is it ethical for me to give it to you if I have doubts about your ability to return it?

If there is an expectation of reciprocity, how can I give you something that I'd like you to have without expecting anything in return? If I accept something from you with an intention to pay it back and discover, through circumstances beyond my control, that I can't reciprocate, what is my moral obligation? How does any of this affect our relationships with one another and our sense of self-worth?

If I loan money to someone I know, what is my motivation for doing this? Is it to enable a worthwhile use of my savings, or is it money I would otherwise spend? Is it primarily to be of use to someone who is in need, or is my eye firmly fixed on having it returned? Under what circumstances is it right for one person's debt to be transferred to somebody else? When does my brother's or sister's debt become mine? Should I have a choice about whether or not to take it on? Are the circumstances under which it was incurred relevant?

Gift Economies

Throughout most of human history, people simply shared food with others in their family, clan, or village. Many traditional societies employed practices for redistributing wealth by giving gifts. Such traditions bound people together in mutual relationships and obligations. According to Anthropologist David Graeber, early agricultural economies were "gift economies" in the sense that people exchanged what they had with each other for what they needed, and the obligations created in gift economies were personal, communal, and enduring.[4]

These gift economies were usually cooperative, in the sense of being based on mutual obligations to share the work and its fruits with others in hunter-gatherer and peasant farming communities. In some cultures, as along the Pacific Coast of North America for example, social standing was based on "competitive generosity," and the inability to reciprocate by matching or exceeding the value of gifts one received was a source of shame and loss of status.

10

The idea of sharing profits is undoubtedly very old, and might be seen as a natural extension of the ways in which people traditionally shared food from a successful hunt or harvest. In pre-urban agricultural societies, what was loaned (seeds, animals, and tools) had the power of generation within itself, and the concept of interest could simply have developed from having an interest in sharing the food obtained by working with shared or borrowed seeds, animals, and tools.

Graeber concludes that the use of money began to change the nature of debt from a sense of obligation that was personal, communal, and generalized to one that became impersonal, contractual, and specific. It was also when borrowing and lending became monetized and the payment of debts became part of legal systems. This was when paying something extra in return for using someone else's money began to take hold, and that justice in borrowing and lending became a moral and religious consideration. At what point does gaining more from someone else's labor than they themselves gain become unfair, and thus immoral?

The Early History of Usury and Interest

Earning a return on financial investments has become so commonplace in contemporary Western culture that it can be challenging to imagine that this has not always been the case. Why has charging interest not been universally practiced? Usury today is defined as lending money at exorbitant or illegal rates of interest. Until the 16th century, charging interest in any amount for lending money was called "usury." While usury has been practiced for thousands of years, it has also been vigorously criticized on moral, ethical, religious, economic, and legal grounds.

In Judaism, the Hebrew word for interest is neshekh, which literally means "a bite." The Torah, which governed the Hebrews as a tribal society, strictly forbids usury, by which was meant that Jews were forbidden to charge interest on loans to other Jews, and with only one exception it discouraged receiving interest from strangers as well.

The Torah also recognized the dangers of extensive indebtedness, even when no interest was charged. It called for a "jubilee year" every 49 years (seven times seven Sabbath years) when debts were cancelled and land was returned to its original (tribal) ownership. A number of other early mid-Eastern societies had similar restrictions on usury.

With the growth of cities and hierarchically structured societies in western Asia, metal-based money economies emerged. Usury began to be charged on metals, with interest paid in more metal. This development was a significant change, since interest paid in coinage required that the borrower have a means to acquire coinage. Farmers had to sell their produce or their labor for coinage to participate in the new market economies, and they often fared poorly in exchange. They were sometimes helped by authorities who assigned monetary value to agricultural goods and occasionally forgave debt. Indeed, Solon's reforms of 594 BCE in Athens, which inaugurated the evolution of Athenian democracy, was in many ways akin to the Hebrew's jubilee year.

Aristotle (384-322 BCE) formulated the classical view against usury, saying

> *"Money was intended to be used in exchange but not to increase at interest. And this term interest, which means the birth of money from money, is applied to the breeding of money because the offspring resembles the parent. Wherefore of all modes of getting wealth, this is the most unnatural. [Of those who] "take more than they ought, and from the wrong sources, . . . what is common to them is evidently a sordid love of gain. . ."* [5]

Early Christian Church leaders echoed Aristotle and the Torah, saying that money was a measure and not a means to an end. They also had the words of Jesus to support this position: "lend without expecting any return" (*Luke* 6:35).[6] Pope Leo the Great (440-461) laid the cornerstone for later usury laws when he forbade clerics from taking usury and condemned laymen for it.[7] The prohibition of usury in Islam was well established during the Prophet Mohammed's life, and was reinforced by various of his teachings in the Holy Quran. The prohibition of usury has remained a well-established working principle integrated into the Islamic economic system.[8]

In early and medieval Christian thought, the love of money, not the use of money itself, was said to be "the root of all evil things" (1 *Timothy* 6: 10). These views echo Aristotle's critique of usury as "a sordid love of gain." In the eighth century under Charlemagne, usury was declared to be a general criminal offence.[9] The Lateran Council of 1179 declared that usurers should be ex-communicated.[10]

The Transition to Current Practice

Late in the Middle Ages, as economies became more dynamic, it grew harder to argue that charging interest on business loans where the borrowing merchant prospered was an act of greed or lack of charity. The Lateran Council of 1515 declared that "the proper interpretation of usury [is] when gain is sought from the use of a thing, not in itself fruitful (such as a flock or a field) without labor, expense or risk on the part of the lender."[11]

John Calvin dropped the usury ban in 1536, accepting it as legitimate in business loans, but he still considered usury sinful if it hurt one's neighbor.[12] In Europe, usury came to be understood as excessive interest, and it passed from being an offence against public morality, which a Christian government was expected to suppress, to being a matter of private conscience. The element of risk soon became a justification for charging interest, and the idea of a lending institution charging interest for its services became widely accepted.

The Church in England made the distinction in 1545, when Henry VIII adopted the first statute to legalize moderate usury. In due course, the word "usury" became differentiated from charging interest — rather, usury was taking unfair advantage.[13] Buddhist and Hindu texts also reveal earlier prohibitions of usury that were later diluted to warn against excessive interest.[14]

On the scientific front, in 1610 Francis Bacon, roundly condemned Aristotle's position as dogmatic, yet felt that

"Usury is a thing allowed by reason of the hardness of men's hearts. For since there must be borrowing and lending, and men are so hard of heart as they will not lend freely, usury must be permitted. . . ."[15]

Adam Smith framed interest in economic terms that sound familiar in the 21st century and form part of the foundation of today's world economy:

"The interest or the use of money...is the compensation which the borrower pays to the lender, for the profit which he has an opportunity of making by the use of the money. Part of that profit naturally belongs to the borrower who runs the risk and takes the trouble of employing it; and part to the lender, who affords him the opportunity of making this profit."[16]

Smith viewed the accumulation of financial wealth by lending at interest as the means by which entrepreneurs were able to increase the economy's stocks of real capital, and thus to increase its productivity. Yet he also favored the imposition of an interest rate ceiling, so that those with money would loan to borrowers who were likely to undertake socially beneficial investments, rather than holding out for higher rates that only investors in risky speculative ventures would undertake.

The great twentieth century economist John Maynard Keynes spoke of the need to encourage economic efficiency while keeping the rate of interest down, and suggested "a wise government is concerned to curb [interest] by statute and custom and even by invoking the sanctions of the Moral Law." This seems to have been the perspective that guided the U.S. government's economic policies from the end of the Second World War until the 1960s.[17]

Interest and Discounting

Interest is fundamentally linked to what is known as "discounting the future." From the perspective of an individual, interest is a future gain that may be large enough to lead one to defer current spending. We may save $100 today so that we will receive $105 a year from now, or with compound interest receive $200, double the amount, in 14 years. In conventional economic terms, however, an assumption of economic growth, technical progress, and depreciation/ obsolescence suggests that current assets will be less valuable in the future than they are in the present. "Discounting" the future provides a framework for converting the current value of goods and services into projected future values.

Conventionally, both interest and discount rates are set at a fixed percent per year. While modest fixed-percent interest rates generate exponential growth surprisingly quickly, modest discount rates imply that benefits occurring a decade or two into the future have nearly negligible present value. Even discount rates of only one or two percent lead many conventional economists to conclude that it's wiser to invest in making the next generations wealthy enough to cope with changing climate than to spend money today to forestall future climate disasters.

Ecological economists and other critics see discounting as ethically flawed for failing to recognize the preferences and choices of future generations as having equal value to those of present generations. They see it as conceptually flawed for failing to recognize that the human economy is embedded within the natural environment. For example, higher discount rates justify consuming non-renewable natural resources ever faster, yet this economic growth is generally reducing, not increasing, the amount of fresh water, clean air, and natural resources available to the future, all of which are an integral component of wealth. Research on alternatives to established discounting theory are an active area of inquiry.[18]

We are Currently Faced with a Debt Issue of Biblical Proportions

All religious traditions have struggled to distinguish the helpful loan from the oppressive. Put simply, the poor tend to borrow money for necessities, not to finance unaffordable luxuries. Repaying loans is an extra burden on those who lack sufficient income to make ends meet; debt may increase beyond the possibility of repayment as even modest interest charges can accumulate dramatically over time. Since the 1980s, the profusion of credit cards has led to a huge accumulation of household debt that was even larger than government debt in 2009, but has now been surpassed by government debt.

When interest from savings is received and spent, it facilitates economic activity. But when interest from savings is added to savings over a period of years, it leads to the exponential accumulation of savings that drives indiscriminate economic growth and redistributes wealth. When interest on debt is paid on a regular basis, it also facilitates economic activity. But when interest on debt is added to debt, it leads to the exponential accumulation of what often becomes insurmountable debt.

Compound interest in the face of adversity defines the cruelty of usury. As the restraints against usury have steadily weakened, the cruelty of usury has come to be called "predatory lending." In recent years, predatory lending in its extreme form has become a growth industry. It has become an integral component of economic policies that promote private gain at the expense of the common good, and an economic system that requires steadily increasing aggregate debt to sustain itself.

Jesus' parable of the talents has been frequently cited as conveying God's mandate to profit from financial investment.[19] More recently, however, some Biblical scholars have asserted that Jesus' hearers would have known it to be an unmistakable portrayal and condemnation of the behavior of wealthy.[20] The 1989 statement of Pope John Paul II that "capital needed by the debtor nations to improve their standard of living now has to be used for interest payments on their debts" helped support the millennial Jubilee Campaign to eliminate the devastating social impact of the third world debt.[21]

Quaker John Woolman was insightful about the issues of economic exploitation and right relationship. In his *Plea for the Poor* of the 1700s, he writes that it isn't right that poor people work long hours and tire themselves out so that others might have luxuries that only separate them from God.[22]

Whatever religious, philosophical, or ethical views one holds on lending at interest, many indicators point to the conclusion that contemporary levels of debt, much of which has been incurred through predatory lending, have become a major scourge. For example:

- When the recent housing bubble burst, big banks got government bailouts, but they didn't help citizens whose mortgages the banks wrote, bundled, and sold in single-minded pursuit of profit.

- Millions of Americans now owe more on their homes than those homes are worth, and thousands have lost their homes through foreclosure.

- Students are leaving college saddled with a level of debt that would have been unthinkable a generation ago — with ever-shrinking job possibilities to pay it off.

- Credit card companies use sophisticated advertising to create consumer debt, and cut legal corners to extract the maximum they can.

- Predatory lending has left whole countries in debt to foreign banks and international financial institutions, which then impose austerity measures on already impoverished societies.

- While economists worry and politicians rant, corporate and consumer debt rival government debt, making the nation's economic future hostage to creditors.

- In our current system, interest on existing debt can only be paid by creating new debt in steadily increasing amounts, which makes growth an imperative in order for the system to maintain itself.

- The world is living beyond its means, using resources faster than they can be renewed, creating a massive debt to the future.

Conclusion

Borrowing and lending have raised ethical questions for millennia. The modern, Western world has slowly developed norms around lending, based on an evolving understanding of the social value of investment as a means for bringing future prosperity. Yet, disparities of wealth, financial meltdowns, inordinate debt, and evident signs of dysfunctionality in the world economy all indicate that contemporary understanding of finance and investment is neither complete nor entirely accurate. The next three chapters examine the role of savings and investment in the economy and how the economic system has changed since the end of World War II.

Views on the Greek Financial Crisis

The 2015 financial crisis in Greece has generated considerable news coverage and political commentary. Notably, many commenters agree that the causes of the financial crisis in Greece are largely rooted outside Greece itself.

In "We are all Greeks now," Chris Hedges sees comparisons within the United States.[23]

"The poor and the working class in the United States know what it is to be Greek. They know underemployment and unemployment. They know life without a pension. They know existence on a few dollars a day. They know gas and electricity being turned off because of unpaid bills. They know the crippling weight of debt...

"The Greeks and the U.S. working poor endure the same deprivations because they are being assaulted by the same system—corporate capitalism. There are no internal constraints on corporate capitalism. And the few external constraints that existed have been removed. Corporate capitalism, manipulating the world's most powerful financial institutions, including the Eurogroup, the World Bank, the International Monetary Fund and the Federal Reserve, does what it is designed to do: It turns everything, including human beings and the natural world, into commodities to be exploited until exhaustion or collapse. In the extraction process, labor unions are broken, regulatory agencies are gutted, laws are

---

written by corporate lobbyists to legalize fraud and empower global monopolies, and public utilities are privatized...

"Human life is of no concern to corporate capitalists. The suffering of the Greeks, like the suffering of ordinary Americans, is very good for the profit margins of financial institutions such as Goldman Sachs. It was, after all, Goldman Sachs—which shoved subprime mortgages down the throats of families it knew could never pay the loans back, sold the subprime mortgages as investments to pension funds and then bet against them—that orchestrated complex financial agreements with Greece, many of them secret. These agreements doubled the debt Greece owes under derivative deals and allowed the old Greek government to mask its real debt to keep borrowing. And when Greece imploded, Goldman Sachs headed out the door with suitcases full of cash.[23]

In "Grexit or Jubilee," *Ellen Brown argues that the Greek debt could be easily annulled:*

"It is quite possible to grant debt relief, however, without hurting the bondholders. U.S. banks were bailed out by the U.S. Federal Reserve to the tune of more than $16 trillion in virtually interest-free loans, without drawing on taxes. Central banks have a printing press that allows them to create money at will.

"The ECB has already embarked on this sort of debt purchasing program. In January, it announced it would purchase 60 billion euros of debt assets per month beginning in March, continuing to at least September 2016, for a total of €1.14 trillion of asset purchases. These assets are being purchased through "quantitative easing"—expanding the monetary base simply with accounting entries on the ECB's books.

"The IMF estimates that Greece needs debt relief of €60 billion—a mere one month of the ECB's quantitative easing program. The ECB could solve Greece's problem with a few computer keystrokes."[24]

19

A Tale of Two Debts

After the 2007-08 global economic crash, two European countries—Ireland and Iceland—made very different choices about debt. Both had private banks that had seriously overextended themselves, speculating internationally for profit rather than contributing to the general welfare. As a result of the crash, both economies were in shock and both were faced with enormous liabilities.[25]

In Iceland, urged on by popular pressure, the government decided that it, and the general public, was not responsible for the debts of the banks. These banks had been irresponsible, building up bubble assets that had grown to ten times the worth of the Gross Domestic Product. Iceland let the banks fail, indicted several bankers for financial crimes, and took a series of measures to offer debt relief to ordinary citizens.

In Ireland, the government took on the debts of the banks. Since these were their banks, it was appropriate and responsible to claim their debt as sovereign debt. As a practical consequence, through taxation, every citizen of Ireland took on a share of this debt, at a cost of about 9000 euros per person. With the resultant austerity came a massive transfer of wealth from the lower and middle classes to global capital.

Both economies are recovering, though Iceland is struggling with inflation and Ireland is enduring service cutbacks and high unemployment. But the larger questions remain. Was one of these responses more moral? To whom are we obligated, and for what?[25]

CHAPTER 3
Savings, Investment, and Interest in Economic Theory

In nations where western banking and financial practices prevail, borrowing and lending at interest is a normal and accepted component of both business and personal life. In this chapter we will describe the essential roles of savings, investment, and debt in the basic theoretical model of contemporary market economies. We will also explain how bank lending has become the main source of the currency that market economies require to function. We will not discuss the mathematical relationships that economic theory uses to describe the systemic complex of production, consumption, savings, investment, and prices.

Loans provide businesses with the financial capital to build new factories, open new restaurants, and renovate older buildings. Loans make it possible for households to purchase homes, buy cars, pay for college, and cope with emergencies.

When a business or household borrows money, the loan is repaid over a specified amount of time with an additional payment for the use of the money, known as "interest." This monetary return to the lender, in excess of the original amount of the loan, becomes part of the lender's income.

The interest from household savings is often automatically added to savings, which then accumulates steadily as interest is also paid on interest, a process known as "compound interest." For many of us, this is the only way to accumulate enough money to pay for college or provide income for retirement.

Using savings to accumulate financial assets has become so much a part of our culture that we rarely ask, "From where does the income from financial assets come? How does income from financial assets relate to our economic system as a whole? How do the levels of debt and inequality of income and wealth relate to the damage to local and global ecological systems that are so much on many Friends' minds and hearts?" In the next sections we will address these questions.

Earnings from Savings: From Where Do They Come?

The basic model of market activity is a circular flow diagram, in which there are two elements, businesses and households. Businesses pay wages and salaries to households in exchange for labor to make goods and services. Households use earnings from businesses to buy the goods and services that businesses produce.

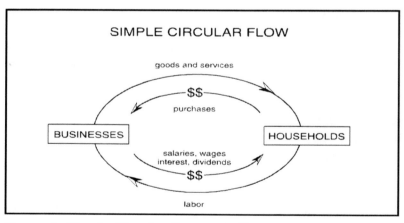

Figure 1. Simple Circular Economic Flow

Missing from this circular flow diagram is the role of banking and finance to make household savings available to businesses and other households, and thus to provide income from savings.

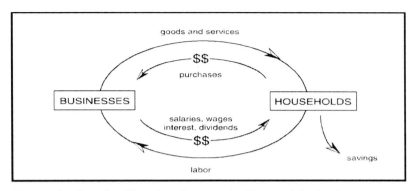

Figure 2. Simple Circular Economic Flow with Savings

There are five basic ways of earning income from savings:

1) interest that banks pay to depositors;
2) distributions that mutual funds pay to share-holders;
3) dividends that corporations pay to shareholders (or profits that businesses make for their owners);
4) interest that businesses or governments pay to bondholders;
5) rent that renters pay to property-owners;

Yet another way to increase savings is to buy financial assets or real property at a time when they seem under-priced, and sell them at a higher price when conditions change. This source of income is called "capital gain," and the process of acquiring it is called "speculation." This income comes either from someone else's earnings or from financial speculation.

Investment and Economic Activity

The explanation for the Great Depression developed by British economist John Maynard Keynes became central to economic theory in the years following World War II. It involves the interplay among savings, investment, unearned income, and maldistribution of wealth, investment, and unearned income. Keynes' perspective helps to explain how the transfer of wealth to those with savings and financial assets affects the system as a whole and leads to his views about the ways government could help prevent future breakdowns of economic activity.[26]

For economists, the technical meaning of "investment" is spending on real capital—the structures, equipment and infrastructure used to produce and distribute goods and services, which are also called "capital goods." Businesses invest by purchasing capital goods to improve and increase the consumer goods they sell to households.

To explain the Great Depression, Keynes focused on a fundamental difficulty with the simplicity of the circular flow diagram. When households save some of their income, not enough money will be spent to buy what businesses produce. If this happens, businesses will produce less and hire fewer workers, who will earn less money to spend, buy less of what businesses produce, and so forth.[26]

The solution to this difficulty is for savings to be restored to the circular flow through the banking and financial systems. When household savings are used to acquire financial assets, they theoretically become available either to businesses to invest in equipment, factories, etc., or to other households to invest in a house, car, education, etc., which increase the household's ability to produce. In theory, more investment creates more jobs. As long as all savings get returned to the circular flow by what businesses and households borrow and spend, the cycle of market activity will continue, and society will prosper.

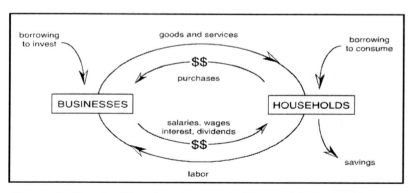

Figure 3. Simple Circular Economic Flow with Borrowing

24

In economic theory, a prosperous economy is a growing economy and vice versa. This is because when businesses or households borrow, they produce more and earn more to pay back their loans. Yet it is easy to see that the circular flow is vulnerable to being interrupted if there are more household savings than businesses and households are willing to borrow.

Earned and Unearned Income

The U.S. Legal Code has traditionally differentiated between "earned" and "unearned" income. Earned income is payments and in-kind benefits people receive in exchange for work or service through employment and self-employment. Unearned income is payments or in-kind benefits that people receive without being required to perform work or service. This typically means interest from savings and loans, dividends from shares of ownership, rent from leased property, and capital gains from the sale of financial assets and real estate.

Different tax policies apply to earned and unearned income. In the 1950s and 1960s, most unearned income was taxed at 25 percent, which for some tax-payers might have been a higher rate than earned income. More recently, for many people, earned income is taxed at a higher rate than unearned income because social security and wage taxes have increased for working people and higher income tax rates have been reduced considerably.

As the financial markets have come to have a more dominant role in the economy overall, returns on financial assets became favored on the increasingly dubious assumption that they help to create jobs and promote economic growth that serves the common good. These "earnings" are no longer referred to with the negative connotation of "unearned," even though the differentiation remains in the tax laws and highlights the ethical issues involved.

Earned and Unearned Income

The reality of earned versus unearned income hit me hard while I was a Maryknoll Lay Missioner in Brazil. I was living and working with recyclers in the municipal dump of Joao Pessoa, a city on the eastern tip of the country. In the dump more than 600 people, including at least 125 children, worked day and night pulling out recyclable materials from the garbage as it poured out of trucks. Most of the year, they worked under the intense tropical sun with dust and smoke from spontaneous fires constantly filling the air. During the rainy season they worked in mud up to their knees, so deep that the garbage trucks often needed to be towed out of the muck.

They worked long hours to sell the materials for pennies per pound. I was amazed and impressed by their diligence and perseverance in continuing to work day after day in such difficult conditions. The reality was that they couldn't miss a day of work because most lived day to day, buying the food for today from the money they earned yesterday. So if they missed a day of work, they often wouldn't eat the next day. Sick days, weekends, vacations didn't exist for them.

After living there for close to two years, helping the recyclers to create a cooperative to improve their working conditions and pay, I was on the phone with my father. He told me that my investments were doing very well. With the overwhelming reality that I was experiencing, I had completely forgotten that before I came to Brazil my dad suggested that I start a retirement fund which I did with the $1,500 that I had in savings plus $500 from my parents to complete the $2000 minimum investment in the Pax World Fund, a socially responsible fund.

Turns out that while my neighbors were working long, difficult hours to barely get by, my "investment" had given me an income almost equal to what they made working in the dump. The only difference being that I did absolutely nothing to earn this income (I had forgotten that it even existed!) while my friends deserved much more than they earned.

—*Dave Kane*

Maldistribution

Keynes' basic explanation for the cause of the Great Depression was a dearth of investment caused by maldistribution of income and wealth, by which he meant that too few people had too much money. Maldistribution results from the massive difference between the income of wage and salary-earners and the income of the wealthy few as unearned income from dividends and other forms of profit. The problem with maldistribution is that most unearned income accrues to those who are already using much of their income for saving rather than spending, and maldistribution increases.[26]

As more and more is being saved by those who already have too much, more and more must be invested by business on capital goods to maintain economic activity. When many households have less to spend than they need because of maldistribution, they are unable to buy the goods and services that businesses are already producing, and there is little reason for businesses to invest.

Sooner or later economic activity will spiral downward because the mass of consumers together earns far less than the value of what they produce and the total value of consumer demand will be less than the total value of the consumer goods produced. Households won't be able to spend enough on consumption to sustain production, and businesses won't spend enough on investment to provide jobs and absorb the ever-increasing "savings" of the wealthy. Without investment in real capital (the physical means of production), economic activity simply disintegrates, which is what happened in the Great Depression.

Earnings and the Trade Cycle

Keynes saw the trade cycle depression as an excess of saving not going to investment with consequent lack of income generation to spur demand. He gave valid policy advice advocating for public works programs to boost spending. But he equated saving with not spending and missed the heart of the problem.[26]

The trade cycle is driven by the failure of white- and blue-collar workers to earn the market worth of their production, leading to falling consumer demand, falling prices, and disincentive for investment. It has been thus for 150 years.

Increasing consumer debt kept the economy going—until debt stopped growing and the economy collapsed. With massive credit card debt failing to increase as borrowers were unable to service and repay, the recent collapse was inevitable. The banks had, with unconscionable irresponsibility, reduced their liquidity ratios from prudent 1:10 or so, to 1:35, even 1:50. Their desperate concern after the crash was to recover liquidity so there was no lending available to spur a recovery.

Unfortunately, governments rejected Keynes' public works approach. The recent depression was not caused by interest rates or debt, rather by the cessation of debt increase. The banks aided and abetted the growth of boom-bust collapse but did not cause it. Their irresponsibility aggravated the pain (foreclosures, derivatives, etc.), but they were not the primary cause.

The American Friends Service Committee's *Putting Dignity at the Heart of the Global Economy* cites *Bloomberg Business* reporting that Costco gets more profit from its workers from a high wage policy than does Walmart with its low wages. Costco is therefore seen to be congratulated for doing the fair thing and benefiting from it. The figures that were cited for the margin of profit attributable per worker are $13,647 for Costco and $11,039 per year for Walmart. Falling demand is not because the workers are saving too much—rather, they are not getting enough to buy what they produce.[27]

Inequality is not simply immoral in itself. It causes a whole range of social harms. Insecurity creates societal tension and moral regression as individuals vie for self-preservation. It also creates a pervasive lack of felt safety and felt belonging as a respected member of a mutual care community. Inequality is a prime indicator of social sickness, a driver of social tension and violent regression.[28]

—Leonard Joy

A Mixed Economy

What did Keynes propose to prevent future depressions? He pointed out that governments function both as businesses and as households. They hire workers and pay salaries and wages; and they buy goods and services from businesses. Governments can prevent the breakdown of the system by acting as a "countervailing force" in the economy to moderate the effects of maldistribution that results from unrestrained market activity.[29]

There are several ways to do this. One way is to place higher taxes on higher incomes. Another, when there is a risk of recession due to insufficient private sector demand, is for the government to increase demand by hiring more and spending more to invest in public goods, and taxing less so businesses and households have more to spend. Similarly, if market activity is flowing and growing, government should hire less, spend less, and tax more to keep the rate of growth from becoming unsustainable.

Understanding that government has an important role in promoting economic activity is what mid-century economists meant by a mixed economy—one in which there is a mix of market activity and government intervention that stabilizes the overall level of economic activity. Otherwise, according to Keynes, market activity on its own would, sooner or later, become unstable, leading either to boom and then bust, or bust without boom.

Money, Interest, and Economic Activity

Keynes advocated that government be a "countervailing force" in managing the economy's money supply through its central bank, the Federal Reserve Bank in the U.S., or the "Fed."[29] The Fed was established in 1913 and strengthened in the 1930s to provide stability to the vitally important, but periodically chaotic, banking system.[30]

Contrary to popular opinion, the Fed is not an agency of the federal government, but a public-private partnership owned by its private member banks. Most of our money supply is not created by the government, even though the

Treasury Department prints our bills and mints coins. All dollar bills are in fact Federal Reserve Notes for which the Treasury Department is paid four cents per bill by the Fed.

One might think the money that banks lend to borrowers is the same money they receive from their depositors, but this is far from the whole story. Most of the trillions of U.S. dollars are created by banks through the time-honored practice of "fractional reserve banking," meaning that banks are required to have in their possession only a fraction of what they are allowed to loan.

The current reserve requirement is around one-twentieth, or five percent, which is why more than 95 percent of the money supply has been created as loans by the banking system. The Fed holds some of the required reserves of its member banks, and the member banks can borrow from the Fed to increase the amounts they are able lend.

When a bank makes a loan it simply credits the borrower's account with the amount of the loan, and the borrower can then write checks against that account. When the borrower uses the loan to write a check to a seller, who puts it in his account, the seller's bank now has an additional deposit so it can make additional loans.

This is "the multiplier effect" of fractional reserve banking. More generally, "the multiplier effect is an economic term referring to how an increase in one economic activity can cause an increase throughout many other related economic activities."[31]

Bank money functions as currency with much more convenience and vastly more frequency than bills and coins. Thus, through the fractional reserve system, the banks determine the money supply as an outcome of the loans they make to borrowers. This feature of our financial system is generally not well understood, and the banking industry is not eager to explain it. It means that for every $1 one of us has on deposit, our bank can earn interest on more than $20 by creating money in the form of loans. Economist John Kenneth Galbraith has written:

"The process by which banks create money is so simple that the mind is repelled," and "To pay off (all) debt (is) to destroy the money supply."[32]

Fractional reserve banking is one example of a general phenomenon in which growth in one business or economic sector stimulates growth in supply sectors and in consumer demand as employees use their earnings for purchases. Bank money functions as currency with much more convenience and vastly more frequency than bills and coins. Since banks make profits on loans, they promote borrowing and thus increase the money supply in response to the demand for loans.

Furthermore, the federal government finances the national debt through the banking system by selling short and long term bonds, on which it pays interest. This means that somewhere in the system interest is being paid by a borrower on almost every dollar in circulation. It means there is a steady systematic transfer of money from borrowers to lenders, which includes taxpayers paying interest to bond-holders for all government debt, which also makes banking a very profitable business. Henry Ford once said:

"It is well enough that people of the nation do not understand our banking and monetary system, for if they did, I believe there would be a revolution before tomorrow morning."[33]

The relationship between the national money supply and the economy's productivity determines the overall price of goods and services, even as specific prices fluctuate. Maintaining stability between the growth of the economy and the increase in the money supply is of great importance. In theory, more money increases economic activity, *i.e.* production, employment, and consumption; but too much money causes inflation, i.e., higher prices.

The Fed manages the money supply indirectly by adjusting the interest rate on its loans to member banks to influence their lending decisions. This also affects the interest rate on government debt that is bought and sold through the banking system and financial markets. Thus, the role and rate of interest is central to the structure of the current monetary system, and thereby of the economy as a whole.

31

Conclusion

Government policy relating to taxation and spending is called "fiscal policy," and government's role through the Fed in influencing the money supply is called "monetary policy." Keynes' policy perspective was that the government should use fiscal and monetary policy to promote high employment, provide for low inflation, and prevent maldistribution of wealth, which he regarded as a major cause of the Great Crash of 1929 and the Great Depression of the 1930s.[34]

With the revival of free market ideology in the 1970s, the language of economics shifted. What had been "unearned income" became "financial earnings." The meaning of investment as spending on real capital, the physical means of production, was lost as investment came to mean the purchase of financial assets.

Maldistribution became "the market failure of insufficient demand." This characterization ignores the systemic reality that too few people with too much money is a detriment to the stability of the economy and society. Instead of having a mixed economy with government playing an important regulatory role, government became viewed as the problem.

We now turn to the way this understanding can be applied to what has happened in the nation's economy as a whole since the end of the Second World War. It can help us understand some of the ways that today's economy is functioning, and some of ways it is failing. Yet our circumstances have changed, so while what Keynes contributed is important, it is no longer sufficient for understanding either our global society's economic dilemmas or the larger context in which the ethical dilemmas of our personal finances are embedded.

CHAPTER **4**

A Political Values Revolution: From Serving the Common Good to Promoting Private Gain

At the heart of humanity's current economic, political, and ecological crises is a fundamental conflict of purpose and moral conviction between promoting private gain and serving the common good. This conflict has been a persistent feature in the market economies of Western Civilization since the Renaissance and Reformation. It has come to manifest in virtually all spheres of society: health, agriculture, education, the media, transport, the legal/penal system, social unrest and violence, militarism, and the environment.

As recently stated by economist-turned-sociologist Juliet Schor, ". . . capitalist economies have a tendency to create inequality. There are exceptions," she said, of which the most notable in the U.S. was after World War II

"when the trauma of war, the power of labor, and the discrediting of free market ideology, led to an unusual period in which government structuring of the market and strong institutional interventions resulted in a time of a growing middle class and declining inequality. But this era we now recognize as unusual, almost an aberration, in a system that excels in accumulating assets and power in the hands of the few."[35]

Steve Frazer describes how "the fables of freedom and politics of fear" have deprived the democratic process of the will and imagination to confront a system run by and for the one percent, and Tea Party zealots have deployed the fervor of old-style populism on behalf of rather than in opposition to corporate domination of the economy.[36]

33

The Post War Period

What made the period following World War II different? Why has the tendency toward inequality returned? Why are we now facing debt issues of biblical proportions?

To consider these questions, it will be helpful to identify some of the ways in which government policies from 1946 to 1968, based more or less on Keynes' analysis and prescriptions, tried to promote the common good.

It was a time of big problems and big changes. In the aftermath of World War II, the GI Bill assisted returning soldiers with education, employment, and housing. The Marshall Plan helped European nations recover from the destruction of war, and a program of technical assistance to developing nations known as Point Four was fore-runner to the Agency for International Development (US AID).

Social Security, and regulation of hours and wages in employment that had been initiated during the 1930s, were strengthened; and the wartime's steeply graduated income tax was largely retained. The construction of the St Lawrence Seaway (with Canada), and the Interstate Highway System were major federal infrastructure projects that benefitted the society at large. In the 1960s, the Peace Corp provided opportunity for many young adults to use their energy and idealism for the common good in other nations and became a signature achievement of President Kennedy.

But not all participated in the post-war prosperity. Racial segregation led to the Civil Rights movement, and poverty, as documented in *The Other America* by Michael Harrington,[37] led to the War on Poverty that became a signature goal of President Johnson.

Medicare, Medicaid, school lunches, and food stamps extended the scope of the social security concept. The Civil Rights and Voting Rights Acts came about because of long-standing abuses and demands to end them that were not limited to southern states. Federal programs to improve the nation's educational system, from pre-school to the university, responded to its obvious inequities. This was all done with very little increase in the federal debt, and a steady decrease

34

in the federal debt as a function of GDP. The marginal tax rate for incomes over $250,000 was as high as 92 per cent until 1965.

Under the mixed economy of Keynesian capitalism, for the two decades after World War II the government was understood to have an important role in the economy as a whole. The banking and financial systems operated within regulations that grew out of the financial crises and bank failures of the 1930s. Commercial banks were not permitted to pay interest on demand deposits (checking accounts); they were prohibited from participating in financial markets; and there were ceilings on interest rates. The interest that savings and loan associations could pay depositors was restricted, and their loans were confined to a 50-mile radius (which later increased to 100 miles).

Toward the end of World War II, in a meeting at Bretton Woods, New Hampshire, the United Nations led by Britain and the U.S. established a global banking system. It included the World Bank, the International Monetary Fund, and the Bank for International Settlements, and made the U.S. dollar the international reserve currency. From the mid-1940s to the late 1960s, this system functioned with remarkable stability, to the U. S.' economic advantage.

Even though the U.S. ended the dollar's domestic gold standard in 1933, it maintained the international value of the dollar at $35 per ounce based on gold reserves traditionally stored at Fort Knox, KY. The Federal Reserve System was able to maintain the stability of the dollar, the money supply, and interest rates at home by influencing the activities of the U.S. banking system.

Other nations maintained the international value of their currencies by exchanging them for dollars, which could in turn be exchanged for U.S. gold. The stability of the dollar provided economic stability to the other industrialized nations until late 1960s, when the world economy outgrew the U.S. supply of gold, and the supply of U.S. dollars overseas expanded due to military spending and development aid.

But the seeds of excessive consumerism, dependence on fossil fuels, and focus on economic growth are found in the relative prosperity of the 1950s. The promotion of the automobile and suburban cultures fed the oil crises of the 1970s. Industrial agriculture, petro-chemical, and other technologies were all developed without regard to their ecological effects. It was President Kennedy who promoted economic growth and made the argument that lowering the highest tax rate would increase economic growth and federal government revenue at a time when Republicans were wary of rapid economic growth.[38]

In 1953, President Eisenhower's nominee for Secretary of Defense, Charles Wilson, a former General Motors executive, became famous because he said, "for years I thought that what was good for our country was good for General Motors, and vice versa."[39] In retrospect, the 1950s was a time when many business leaders seemed to recognize that their interests were best served if their employees could buy their products, if they tried to get along with labor organizations rather than trying to destroy them, if they agreed to fund pensions for their employees' retirement, if they tried to gain market share by providing customers with installment plans rather than to profit from high interest payments and late fees.

The American Enterprise Institute and U.S. Chamber of Commerce may claim today that what's good for business is good for America, but most large corporations, financial institutions, and super-wealthy individuals do not act as though what's good for the American people is a priority for them. How has this come about?

The Largely Invisible Transition to a Casino Economy

In the last quarter of the 20th century, policy-makers largely abandoned the role of government as an instrument of human progress. They favored instead an economic philosophy that opposes any government policies that interfere with the profit-seeking of wealthy individuals and large corporations. In the U.S. this has been termed "trickle-down" economics or "Reaganomics," while in most of the world this philosophy is called "neo-liberalism." This ideology is based on many assumptions about markets that have been rendered false by historical developments. Furthermore, the unfettered pursuit of private gain promotes indifference to suffering, and creates obstacles to cultivating ties with family and community, self-actualization through education and vocation, and recognition of global and ecological interdependence. The pursuit of private gain tends to obsess the winners and rob the losers.

Beginning in the 1970s, many interrelated changes occurred that transformed our nation's political landscape and the global financial system to favor private gain. Among them are a corporate counter-reform movement, the end of the international gold standard, the shift toward a free-market ideology, and the application of electronic technologies to financial accounts, transactions, and products.

August of 1971 was a pivotal month for these changes. It was when soon-to-be Supreme Court Justice Lewis Powell sent an extensive memo to a U.S. Chamber of Commerce official about a perceived threat to the interests of big business (*sidebar*). The Powell memo is credited with initiating a well-funded and orchestrated effort to increase the political power of corporations and wealth in reaction to the policies and events of the 1960s. It led to revitalizing the Chamber of Commerce and the American Enterprise Institute, and establishing the Heritage Foundation (1973) and Cato Institute (1977), all to influence academic research, political discourse, and public policy. It led to a huge increase in the number political action committees (PACs) designed to funnel large amounts of money into particular campaign coffers and increased numbers of corporate lobbyists influencing Congress. All of this amounted to a concerted effort to mold the rhetoric in the mass media to conform to the values of private gain.[40]

The Powell Memo

The Powell memo was written in August 1971 by corporate lawyer and future Supreme Court justice Lewis Powell as a discussion piece for the Chamber of Commerce. It urges corporate leaders to respond to the "assault on the enterprise system." In the memo, Powell writes,

"One does not exaggerate to say that, in terms of political influence with respect to the course of legislation and government action, the American business executive is truly the 'forgotten man.'"

He also urges the Chamber to become more politically active:

"Business must learn the lesson ... that political power is necessary; that such power must be assiduously cultivated; and that when necessary, it must be used aggressively and with determination—without embarrassment and without the reluctance which has been so characteristic of American business. ...

"There should be no hesitation to attack the [Ralph] Naders, the [Herbert] Marcuses and others who openly seek destruction of the system. There should not be the slightest hesitation to press vigorously in all political arenas for support of the enterprise system. Nor should there be reluctance to penalize politically those who oppose it."[41]

Only three months after writing this memo, the Senate confirmed Lewis Powell to be a Supreme Court justice. In First National Bank of Boston v. Bellotti (1978), the key forerunner to Citizens United, Justice Powell assembled a bare majority to give corporations and banks the right to spend without limit to influence public opinion. "The inherent worth of the speech in terms of its capacity for informing the public does not depend on the identity of its source," he ruled.

August of 1971 was also when the Nixon Administration unilaterally altered the "Bretton Woods" international financial architecture that had provided economic stability since the end of World War II. U.S. government debt, rather than gold, became the backing for the dollar, which remained as the international reserve currency, even as the dollar's value fluctuated in relation to all other national currencies.

This was ostensibly done to prevent the collapse of the dollar's value because there were no longer enough gold reserves to support it. But it also increased the role of the world's major banks in the soon-to-be globalized financial system.

During the 1970s, much of the dominant economists' voice began to shift toward a neo-liberal, "free market" ideology, claiming that government interference prevents markets from enabling the self-interest of individuals to serve the best interests of the society as a whole.

It was also during the 1970s that computer and internet technologies began to be widely used in the banking and financial sectors. This, coupled with the policies of deregulation, soon led to the creation of electronic money with no reference to any tangible assets, financial markets operating 24 hours a day, seven days a week, and a multi-trillion dollar speculative currency trading industry. The computerization of finance was a major step toward the current system, in which the global money supply is now determined primarily by international financial transactions and is beyond the control of any government.

In the 1980s the neo-liberal economic policies of reducing the taxation of wealth and loosening the regulation of business, banking and finance, came to define the politics of Margaret Thatcher in Great Britain, and Ronald Reagan in the U.S. A symbolic indicator of this shift was the elimination of "maldistribution," "mixed-economy," and "unearned income" from the language of the economics profession.

Now a distinction is often made between the real economy and the financial economy. The real economy is about producing and exchanging goods and services. It uses money to help make and do things that people need and want. The financial economy is about buying and selling stocks, bonds, and a host of recently created financial products in financial markets, which represent claims to dollars, which can be used for goods and services in the real economy.

Buying shares of a company's stock, becoming a part owner, is an investment in the real economy when a reasonable rate of return is expected from producing useful goods and services. But buying a stock to sell as soon as its value goes up is a form of financial speculation. Buying a financial product, the value of which is based on what the future value of something else will be, is pure speculation, somewhat akin to betting on a race horse or sporting event.

The financial economy has great influence in the real economy, and it also promotes speculation—the practice of buying and selling financial instruments to make a profit on their shifting values. Speculation contributes to the accumulation of financial wealth by those who succeed. It can also contribute to the instability of the global financial system, which puts the world's real economy in perpetual risk. John Maynard Keynes, who was a financial speculator, said, "Speculators may do no harm as bubbles on a steady stream of enterprise. But the position is serious when enterprise becomes the bubble in a whirlpool of speculation. When the capital development of a country becomes the by-product of the activities of a casino, the job is likely to be ill-done."[42]

In 1993 economist Joel Kurtzman published *The Death of Money*, which described the way the global monetary and financial systems had changed since the international gold standard was eliminated in 1971. There is irony in his title because the death of the gold-backed dollar, combined with other political, ideological, and technological developments, resulted in a huge increase in the amount of money in circulation and a shift in the ethical values that money represents.[43]

Beginning in the 1930s, government regulations had separated the functions and activities of commercial banks, savings banks, and investment banks, and interest rates on savings accounts and credit cards had been restricted. But in

40

1978, the credit card restrictions were eliminated. Then during the Reagan Administration, banking de-regulation, tax cuts, and increased government debt began to feed the expansion of the financial economy and its effects on the real economy.

In the 1980s, savings bank regulations were substantially reduced, which contributed to the savings and loan scandal of 1989. In 1998, the legal separation between commercial and investment banks was ended, which increased the consolidation and influence of the banking and financial sectors, and contributed to the growth of too-big-to-fail Wall Street banks. Financial speculation became a core activity of most large corporations, leading many critics to refer to the financial economy as "the casino economy."

Kurtzman reported that in 1970, the financial economy was about twice the size of the real economy; that is, the dollar value of all stocks, bonds, and other paper contracts was about twice the dollar value of all goods and services, farms and factories, schools, hospitals, etc. By the 1990s, values in the financial economy had become highly volatile, and fluctuated somewhere between 20 to 50 times as large as the values in the real economy, largely due to the globalization and deregulation of banking and finance, the emergence of "off-shore" banking, and the creation of new financial products derived from speculating on future financial activity.[43]

The casino economy has produced a huge increase in the global money supply, most of which is created through interest-bearing debt via computer transactions—even borrowing for the buying and selling of money itself. There has been much fanfare, with both reason and demagoguery, about the national debt, but currently household debt is nearly as much as government debt, and both are dwarfed by the debt carried in the financial sector.

Almost all this new money accrues to those who participate in the system that creates it. Much of the U.S. population is tied to this system indirectly through insurance policies and pension funds. But its main beneficiaries are wealthy individuals and corporations that trade in financial markets, who also contrive to reduce or evade taxation. This shifts the tax burden to everyone else.

Changes in the income tax rates reduced the maximum tax rate on high incomes and capital gains. After WW II, the top tax rate had continued at its wartime level of about 90 percent. The Kennedy Administration advocated a reduction to about 70 percent, enacted in 1965, to spur capital investment and economic growth, which was also expected to increase government revenue. "A rising tide lifts all boats" was its justification, and at that time increased capital investment did tend to increase employment, wages and revenue.

In the 1980s the Reagan Administration used, or one might say "misused," the same argument and reduced the top tax rate from about 70 percent to just under 30 percent. This led to an unsurprising decrease in revenue. Coupled with an increase in military spending, it produced the nation's first peacetime budget deficits and increase in the national debt.

This was a time when labor unions were under attack, wages were stagnating, and U.S. corporations were beginning to shift investments and manufacturing to other low-wage countries. All these changes were a clear manifestation of the shift in the corporate sector's policy orientation that had begun in the 1970s, from serving the common good to promoting private gain.

It was also when financial markets were expanding much more rapidly than the real economy. Financial speculation was encouraged by a reduction in the maximum capital gains tax from a high of 40 percent in the late 1970s to 20 percent in 1981. In the mid-1980s, both the top income and capital gains rates were raised somewhat, as a fiscal necessity, until they were reduced to their lowest level in modern times during the second Bush Administration.

Speculation in financial markets tends to create bubbles of false asset values which sooner or later must burst. The "dot-com bubble" of the late 1990s burst in 2000-01. The government and financial sector's efforts to offset its threat to the real economy, with the deceptive marketing of "securities" backed by sub-prime mortgages, contributed to the housing bubble which burst in 2007.

As described by Al Gore,

"the global market crisis of 2008 was primarily caused by securitized sub-prime mortgages, hedged with an exotic form of insurance that proved to be illusory. Robo-sourcing these complex financial instruments that no one could possibly understand helped market them to buyers throughout the global economy."[44]

But when the actual quality and real value of the mortgages in question were belatedly examined,

"they were suddenly re-priced on a mass basis . . . bursting the housing bubble.

"The fact that the mortgage-backed securities were linked to a complex web of other computer-driven financial transactions — collateralized debt obligations — led to the credit crisis, a massive disruption in the availability of capital as a basic factor of production in the (real) global economy . . . ."[44]

There are those who hold that the whole financial economy is now sustained by artificial financial products based on bubbles of unpayable debt, which was a major factor in the depth of the "great recession" in the real economy.

Conventional free-market wisdom claims that financial investment creates jobs. Yet in today's financialized economy, many large corporations participate in the financial economy. This does not lead to increased investment in real capital, especially to investment that creates more middle-income jobs, but rather to increased speculation in financial markets.

Impacts of the Casino Economy

In the systemic shift to the casino economy — from "the common good" to "private gain" — those who are wealthy continue to prosper while the rest of us pay the piper. In January, 2015, Oxfam reported that 48 percent of all global wealth is now held by the wealthiest 1 percent, and that next year their share will rise to more than half. A mere 80 individuals, many fewer than in previous years, now own the same amount of wealth as more than 3.5 billion people. And the wealth of these individuals has doubled since 2009.[45] There are limits to how much money billionaires can make use of in their personal lives. So there are vast and steadily growing quantities of financial capital that must find profitable investments in the real economy.

What Happens if One Avoids Going into Debt?

My wife and I decided we needed to move from our home of 27 years, that we own free and clear, to a house and location that is more suited to aging in place. We've chosen a location and want to buy a house there before we sell our current home. This means getting a mortgage that we will pay down with the proceeds from the sale of our home.

We've applied to a number of lending institutions for a mortgage. We can't qualify with any of them, because we have no credit rating since we have no debt. We've learned that federal regulations require a credit rating to qualify for a mortgage. We've tried to avoid debt and pay for what we buy and owe with cash, check, or debit card. Although we have retirement savings that exceed the amount of the mortgage we need, we can't access them to buy a house without creating a large tax obligation to both the IRS and NJ-TGI.

The apparent solution is to acquire two credit cards on separate accounts and apply for a line of credit, all of which we're able to do at our credit union, and make use of them for at least three months. But we may only qualify for "secured" credit cards, which requires providing the credit union with cash in the amount of the line of credit we want for each card, plus an annual fee for each card of $59.

Not only does our economy require debt to function. So does anyone who needs to borrow.

Here's the debt trap at work. We've avoided debt and only want to get a mortgage because it's to our advantage. So for us it's only an inconvenience, though a rather large one. But what about people who have to borrow? They're a feast for predatory lenders.

The whole economy is at risk if people can't pay their debts, so a lot of financially insecure people are a threat to the system. Yet the system is in the business of increasing the financial insecurity of a great many people.

This is crazy!

—Ed Dreby

Some negative trends are:

- Investing in political power through the funding of lobbyists and think tanks, ownership of media, and spending on political campaigns.

- Privatizing public and non-profit functions, promoted by depriving the public sector of revenue: home mortgage programs in 1968, followed by health insurance, hospitals, scientific research, municipal services, social services, schools and colleges, and even prisons and military services.

- Increasing profits by investing in automation, robotics, and artificial intelligence to reduce labor costs by eliminating jobs.

- Promoting predatory lending on a systemic scale by promoting credit cards, sub-prime mortgages, secondary mortgages, student debt, etc., and a profusion of collection agencies.

- Privatizing the bio-productivity of nature and its genetic codes by creating new "markets" to buy and sell water, biodiversity, plant and animal species and carbon emissions.

Rather than increasing general well-being, such investments create distortions in the real economy and degrade overall quality of life. A particularly egregious example is the sale of military equipment to police departments, which, from the vendors' perspective, represents a promising new market. Such equipment is then available to quell social unrest and to fill privatized prisons with new inmates. With or without military equipment, when profits can be made from locking people up—youth in detention facilities, immigrants in holding centers, minorities in prisons—then those people can be seen as simply the raw material required for a business activity. It is sobering to understand how far the financial sector has come in mining the real economy for ever-increasing investment opportunities, regardless of human cost, and with no thought for the common good.

Conclusion

The trajectory of change in the national and global economies that began in the 1970s continues unabated. It has led to our current conditions of extreme economic inequality, political domination by a global economic elite, subservience of the real economy to the interests of the financial sector, extensive privatization of formerly public and non-profit functions and services, explosion of household debt and systemic predatory lending.

All this has increased economic insecurity for a great many people, and made choices and decisions about how to use one's savings more varied, complex, and ethically problematic. And yet, before we turn to consideration of options for promoting individual economic security, we must widen the lens even farther, to look at our relationship with the biosphere. Our current economic and political institutions, whether focused on serving private gain or the common good, all have an assumption of the existence of unlimited resources and the necessity of economic growth. The arc of these underlying assumptions leads to a future of enormous insecurity for humanity as a whole, greatly intensifying the conflict between promoting private gain and serving the common good. Having a better grasp of these dynamics will help clarify the basis on which we make our decisions.

CHAPTER 5
Environmental Limits
on Economic Growth

An understanding of the way in which our economic system is embedded in the biosphere began to emerge in the 1960s. This was when damage to the environment first became a widespread concern; when limits to economic growth began to be considered; when future climate disruption from burning fossil fuel began to be anticipated by climate scientists; and it is now known to be when humanity's ecological footprint began to exceed the Earth's bio-capacity.

In 1973, a team of young MIT computer modelers published *The Limits to Growth*, about projections of exponential economic and population growth in a world of finite resources.[47] That same year, Herman Daly, a young establishment-trained economist, began to promote the idea of "steady-state economics" as an ecological necessity on a finite planet.[46]

Over time, Daly's initiative led to the development of ecological economics as an independent academic field that challenges the foundations of orthodox economics.[47] Yet the firestorm of fierce criticism directed at *The Limits to Growth* from the corporate public relations establishment led those who shared this understanding to be marginalized and ignored for many years.

Energy, Economics,
and Sustainable Development

In the early 1970s, domestic oil production began to decline, so the U.S. economy became heavily dependent on oil imports. This made both the U.S. and world economies much more dependent on the Organization of Petroleum Exporting Countries (OPEC), and the price of oil more than doubled between 1970 and 1980.

Oil price increases helped fuel predatory lending on a global scale, as many oil producing nations received a great deal of money, much of which was deposited in large U.S. banks. During the 1970s, the World Bank concentrated on lending for projects intended to meet the basic needs of people in the developing world. This led the banks to make massive loans to often-corrupt political regimes in developing nations, leading to the rapid rise of Third World debt, which from 1976 to 1980 increased at a 20 percent average annual rate.[48]

Then the doubling of oil prices and rising interest rates made it a lot more difficult for many developing nations to meet their debt obligations. In 1982, the World Bank adopted a neo-liberal ideological focus that emphasized lending to developing nations to service their debts, and imposed structural adjustment policies designed to streamline their economies by privatizing services and cutting social programs.[49]

UNICEF reported in the late 1980s that the structural adjustment programs of the World Bank had been responsible for "reduced health, nutritional and educational levels for tens of millions of children in Asia, Latin America, and Africa." This also forced many developing nations to "liquidate" their natural resources to avoid defaulting on their indebtedness. To this day, more money flows from developing to industrialized nations than from industrialized to developing nations. While industrialized countries send around $130 billion in aid to developing countries each year, that amount is dwarfed by the estimated $900 billion that corporations remove through repatriated profits and tax avoidance plus nearly $600 billion that developing countries send in debt payments.[50]

In 1983, a UN Secretary General's initiative established an independent World Commission on Environment and Development led by former Norwegian prime minister Gro Harlem Brundtland. The Commission's 1987 report, *Our Common Future*, promoted the ideal of "sustainable development."[51]

In the U.S., this led to a number of local and regional sustainable development projects, such as, Sustainable Seattle, which was founded in 1991. Their approach was to identify locally important sustainable development indicators, such as asthma incidence in cities and fish populations in rivers, and then to establish target benchmarks to measure progress. This also led to a variant called "smart growth" which pertained primarily to reducing suburban sprawl, though it also involved cutting costs by promoting greater energy efficiency.[52]

Ecological Economics, Climate Disruption and Political Corruption

By the 1990s, ecological economics began to emerge as a separate field that challenged some fundamental tenets of mainstream economists, led by Herman Daly.[53] Daly regarded Quaker Economist Kenneth Boulding as one of his intellectual mentors. Boulding, speaking to some professional colleagues, once quipped that the only people who believe infinite growth is possible on a finite planet are madmen and economists. He asserted that Earth had become like a spaceship, and economics could no longer be based on an assumption of unlimited resources or a goal of increasing the production and consumption of goods and services.[54]

Daly made a fundamental distinction between economic development, which improves the way resources are used, and economic growth, which increases the quantity of resources used and the rate at which they are degraded. He and other ecological economists have long regarded the idea of "sustainable growth" as an oxymoron.

Charles Eisenstein has spelled out the linkages between the financial economy and unsustainable economic growth in plainer terms than most.

49

"Endless growth means endlessly increasing production and endlessly increasing consumption. Social critics have for a long time pointed out the resulting hollowness carried by that thesis. Furthermore, it is becoming increasingly apparent that infinite growth is impossible on a finite planet. Why, then, are liberals and conservatives alike so fervent in their pursuit of growth?

"The reason is that our present money system can only function in a growing economy. Money is created as interest-bearing debt: it only comes into being when someone promises to pay back even more of it.

"Therefore, there is always more debt than there is money. In a growth economy that is not a problem, because new money (and new debt) is constantly lent into existence so that existing debt can be repaid.

"But when growth slows, good lending opportunities become scarce. Indebtedness rises faster than income, debt service becomes more difficult, bankruptcies and layoffs rise."[55]

Indeed, Eisenstein doesn't even blame the banks:

"In all fairness, we cannot blame the banks for their reluctance to lend. Why would they lend to maxed-out borrowers in the face of economic stagnation? It would be convenient to blame banker greed; unfortunately, the problem goes much deeper than that."[55]

In his opinion it's much more likely that what we are experiencing is the initial birth pains of a no-growth society:

"The problem that we are seemingly unable to countenance is the end of growth. Today's system is predicated on the progressive conversion of nature into products, people into consumers, cultures into markets and time into money. We could perhaps extend that growth for a few more years by fracking, deep-sea oil drilling, deforestation, land grabs from indigenous people and so on, but only at a higher and higher cost to future generations. Sooner or later – hopefully sooner – we will have to transition towards a steady-state or de-growth economy."[55]

What renewed the controversy about limits to growth in the 1990s was climate change and the political conflicts it created. In 1988, prominent U.S. climate scientist James Hansen advised Congress of what had become clear to many scientists: that the most dangerous manifestation of economic growth for the future of civilization was global warming caused by the accumulation of carbon dioxide and other greenhouse gasses due to human activity.[56]

In 1989, the UN and World Meteorological Organization formed the Intergovernmental Panel on Climate Change (IPCC) to periodically assess and report to policy-makers about the scientific consensus on climate change. That same year, science journalist Bill McKibben published *The End of Nature*, the first book for a general audience about global warming.[57] One response was a Framework Convention on Climate Change, negotiated at the Rio Earth Summit in 1992, which was subscribed to by 196 countries.

But, ironically, the most immediate, and to date far more successful response, was the persistent and concerted effort by the fossil fuel industries and their allies to distort the science, confuse the public, and prevent any legislation or negotiations to reduce fossil fuel consumption from succeeding. The dishonesty and deceit involved with these efforts has been repeatedly documented.[58] The Union of Concerned Scientists estimates that more than $1 billion a year, much of it undisclosed, is spent by the fossil industries and their allies, to influence policies and politics on a global scale.[59]

Every time public opinion has shifted toward taking action to address climate change, the corporate interests have launched a targeted counter-offensive to shift it the other way. Most recently, this has occurred in response to Pope Francis' Encyclical. For example, Republican presidential candidate Jeb Bush said, that "the Pope should leave science to the scientists."[60]

The Paris climate change agreement in 2015 was negotiated so that the Obama Administration did not have to submit anything to Congress, but even so Congressional Republicans are determined to undermine the agreement by whatever means they can.[61]

There has been a shameless drumbeat of "jobs versus the environment" and "reducing taxes to create jobs" funded by corporate interests whose demonstrated priority is to increase profits by cutting jobs and reducing labor costs. One of Kenneth Boulding's fears was that our society would become a two-decked spaceship: first class and steerage. This seems to be the direction that a government dominated by unregulated global corporations would take us.

The Tobacco Treaty

Surveys show that between 60 to 80 percent of people in the U.S. think that corporations have too much influence in public policy. Corporate influence in the halls of Congress and regulatory agencies has reached alarming proportions. Fortunately a landmark treaty created by the World Health Organization took on this problem in a significant way by removing the ability for the tobacco industry to participate in policy making.

In 2005 the World Health Organization (WHO) passed the Framework Convention on Tobacco Control, commonly called the "Tobacco Treaty."[62] It is the first legally binding treaty for the WHO and the first-ever public health and corporate accountability treaty. The treaty creates an internationally coordinated response to the tobacco epidemic encouraging governments to raise taxes or prices to discourage tobacco use, put prominent warnings on tobacco packages, and ban tobacco advertising and sponsorship.

Perhaps the most significant part of the Tobacco Treaty is article 5.3 that according to the organization Corporate Accountability International "enshrines in international law the principle that the tobacco industry has no role in public policy." The article states, "In setting and implementing their public health policies with respect to tobacco control, [governments] shall act to protect these policies from commercial and other vested interests of the tobacco industry in accordance with national law."

The article has allowed dozens of countries to implement much stricter policies than would have been possible with the presence of tobacco corporations in policy debates. The treaty is an important precedent that many are trying to implement in other areas. Imagine if the international climate talks were able to take place without the heavy presence of fossil fuel corporations, or if health care policy could be created without pharmaceutical corporations.

The Growth Dilemma

An increasing number of prominent figures in social and environmental policy now realize that the for-profit economic system is on a collision course with Earth's biological and physical realities. They are joining the ecological economists in calling for fundamental changes to our economic institutions so the growth imperative is removed; so that they serve the common good rather than private gain; so that ecological survival takes precedence over economic growth.

The voices calling for an economic system that can adapt to the social and ecological realities of a finite biosphere are beginning to coalesce into a unified movement. Established in 2015, the Next System Project is designed to facilitate systemic changes through webinars, teach-ins, tools, research, and films.[63]

But there is yet to be a shared understanding of what this will require or how it can be done. However, it is clear that adapting to these social and ecological realities will require not only major changes in our economic institutions and technologies, but also a cultural transformation in our personal aspirations and social responsibilities.

We are living in a marketing and media culture that glorifies private gain. Therefore the commonly held assumption about the meaning of "the common good" is "more" for everyone. This is in direct conflict with the realities of the current human-Earth relationship. The common good for human-kind in an ecological context can only be served by using less—a lot less—which is something the economic system as currently structured cannot tolerate.

Conclusion

Neo-liberal ideology that promotes and protects private gain requires systemic corporate and political indifference to societal well-being and ecological integrity. Its current economic and political predominance is causing both social and ecological disintegration. As Chinese philosopher Lao Tse reportedly once said, "If you don't change direction, you'll probably end up where you're headed."[64] Joe Volk, executive director emeritus of FCNL was fond of saying "we live in a now and not yet world."[65]

How do we discern what we must do to live in the "now" world of private gain, while doing what we can to help make the "not yet" world that serves the commonwealth of life a reality? It may not be as difficult to discern ways forward for our personal aspirations, as it is for our dealings with the financial system in which we are embedded. This is the challenge to which we now turn.

What is the Economy For?

Pope Francis spoke about the problems faced by the poor and indigenous peoples at the Second World Meeting of the Popular Movements at the Expo Feria Exhibition Centre in Santa Cruz de la Sierra, Bolivia, on July 9, 2015:

"I know that you are looking for change, and not just you alone: in my different meetings, in my different travels, I have sensed an expectation, a longing, a yearning for change, in people throughout the world. Even within that ever smaller minority which believes that the present system is beneficial, there is a widespread sense of dissatisfaction and even despondency. Many people are hoping for a change capable of releasing them from the bondage of individualism and the despondency it spawns...

"Today, the scientific community realizes what the poor have long told us: harm, perhaps irreversible harm, is being done to the ecosystem. The earth, entire peoples and individual persons are being brutally punished. And behind all this pain, death and destruction there is the stench of what Basil of Caesarea called "the dung of the devil." An unfettered pursuit of money rules. The service of the common good is left behind. Once capital becomes an idol and guides people's decisions, once greed for money presides over the entire socio-economic system, it ruins society, it condemns and enslaves men and women, it destroys human fraternity, it sets people against one another and, as we clearly see, it even puts at risk our common home...

"The first task is to put the economy at the service of peoples. Human beings and nature must not be at the service of money. Let us say NO to an economy of exclusion and inequality, where money rules, rather than service. That economy kills. That economy excludes. That economy destroys Mother Earth.

"The economy should not be a mechanism for accumulating goods, but rather the proper administration of our common home. This entails a commitment to care for that home and to the fitting distribution of its goods among all. It is not only about ensuring a supply of food or "decent sustenance." Nor, although this is already a great step forward, is it to guarantee the three "L's" of land, lodging and labor for which you are working. A truly communitarian economy, one might say an economy of Christian inspiration, must ensure peoples' dignity and their "general, temporal welfare and prosperity." This includes the three "L's," but also access to education, health care, new technologies, artistic and cultural manifestations, communications, sports and recreation.

A just economy must create the conditions for everyone to be able to enjoy a childhood without want, to develop their talents when young, to work with full rights during their active years and to enjoy a dignified retirement as they grow older. It is an economy where human beings, in harmony with nature, structure the entire system of production and distribution in such a way that the abilities and needs of each individual find suitable expression in social life. You, and other peoples as well, sum up this desire in a simple and beautiful expression:"to live well."[66]

CHAPTER 6

Struggling to Save in a Changing World

Gaining a fuller understanding of the dynamics at work in our economic system is a sobering exercise. We are so thoroughly enmeshed in it that our options can seem very limited, and we find ourselves living examples of a conflict between personal values and economic realities. To be responsible parents, family members and contributing citizens, it is hard to see any other choice than to put all the savings we can into financial investments to help pay for our children's education and our own retirement. As responsible trustees of religious, educational, and other non-profit entities, we invest with an eye toward securing the ongoing viability of our valued communities and institutions. We count on the compound interest and hope for high returns.

Yet the system that depends on compound interest in the single-minded pursuit of high returns has lost whatever moral center or restraint it may once have had. An inherently expansionary economic system is straining the capacity of the planet to provide resources and absorb waste to the breaking point. It is increasingly unable to deliver on its promises. Nor do those in positions of economic power seem at all concerned about the common good. To those who are in debt, whose mortgages are under water, or who are being squeezed by cuts in social services and the drive toward privatization, it has become a nightmare.

We were not being squeezed so hard just a few short generations ago. Now that we have a bigger picture of how the financial markets have come to dominate our economy, let us turn our attention to the forces that have set us up to become dependent on them as never before.

56

Post World War II Retirement Plans

Before the 1970s some were benefiting from unearned income through investments and trusts, but they were the more affluent minority. Life insurance policies provided a way that even a working person of modest means could help provide for his (or occasionally her) family in case of death.

Unearned income was part of the economic picture. The stock market was a place for employers to put pension funds, for corporations to raise capital by issuing shares of stock, and for life insurance companies to invest. But ordinary individuals had little personal contact with it. Since the development of federal deposit insurance during the 1930s, bank accounts were secure, and savings at local banks were often channelled into local loans. Even basic retirement needs were met with little personal involvement with unearned income.

It seemed that our retirement system in the United States was secure. Many workers, along with their employers, were paying into public and private tax-deferred pension plans with the assurance of retirement benefits through definedbenefit plans. According to the Employee Benefit Research Institute, from 1940 to 1960, the number of people covered by private pensions increased from 3.7 million to 19 million, or to nearly 30 percent of the labor force, and by 1975, 103,346 plans covered 40 million people.[67] At least two generations grew up under the assumption that if they had a job with an established company, a retirement plan would pay future bills — from the time they retired until their death.

In addition, most of the workforce was paying into the Social Security trust fund — one generation of workers putting in while the one that came before took out. With the advent of Medicare, federal tax dollars were being allocated for the healthcare needs of the elderly. While pension contributions went into investment instruments like mutual funds, the public money was a combination of taxation and forced savings.

A Major Change in the 1970s

This began to change when tax-deferred Individual Retirement Accounts (IRAs) were introduced in 1975 for taxpayers who did not have pension plans. IRAs were soon made available, with an increased annual contribution, to all taxpayers with earned income. In 1978 Congress passed an obscure addition to tax code section 401: 401(k), a modest tax break for companies letting workers put away cash on the side. In 1980 a retirement planner saw unintended potential in 401(k). If workers took some of their own paycheck and set it aside for retirement, they could get extra money from the boss, as well as a tax deferment. This could help convert workers from spenders to savers, and enable them to do something they wouldn't do on their own.[68]

When these "defined **contribution**" plans were first introduced in the late 1970s, they were never intended to replace the traditional "defined **benefit**" plans, but to supplement employer-funded pension and profit-sharing plans, and to thereby provide enhanced retirement security for employees. Since 401(k) participants were presumed to have their basic retirement income needs covered by an employer-funded plan and Social Security, they were given substantial discretion over 401(k) choices, including whether to participate, how much to contribute, how to invest, and when and in what form to withdraw the funds.

But in the early 1980s, 401(k) plans took off, and what had been intended as a supplement to a retirement plan soon became the only retirement plan. The IRS issued regulations sanctioning the use of employee salary reductions as a source of retirement plan contributions. Many employers replaced older, after-tax thrift plans with 401(k)s and added 401(k) options to profit-sharing and stock bonus plans. Within two years, surveys showed that nearly half of all large firms were either offering a 401(k) plan or considering one. The shift from defined benefit plans to defined contribution plans shifted the risk of loss in financial markets from the employer to the employee.

In 1986, Congress acted to replace the defined benefit plan for federal civilian workers with a less generous defined benefit plan and a generous 401(k)-type plan. By this action, the federal government endorsed a shift from a traditional stand-alone defined benefit plan to a combination of a defined benefit plan and a defined contribution plan to which employees could contribute an amount of their choice. It encouraged private-sector employers to be confident about the long-term survivability of 401(k)-type plans. They became popular for small companies that hadn't been able to afford retirement programs and quickly became the fastest-growing type of retirement plan in the United States.

In 1990, 20 million people participated in nearly 100,000 401(k) plans, with total assets of nearly $385 billion. Just six years later, 31 million people were participating in more than 230,000 401(k) plans, with total assets of a trillion dollars, and the numbers have continued to rise.[69]

As they started 401(k) plans, big companies began dropping their traditional pension plans, which were expensive. In 1983 there were 175,143 such plans, but in 2008 there were only 46,926.[70] The 401(k) plans became the primary retirement benefit plans.

It was a huge change. The result shifted the responsibility for managing the pension funds' assets to provide a guaranteed retirement from the employer to the individual. This shifted almost complete discretion and investment risk to individuals. Within a few short years we were catapulted into the era of "do-it-yourself" retirement.[71]

Gambling on Retirement in the Twenty-first Century

401(k) "do-it-yourself" retirement planning hit its stride in the 1990s, and the following decade of bull markets gave the whole idea of basing our security on the speculative markets a series of green lights. But then came the financial crisis of 2007. At a time when more of the population of the United States had stock ownership than ever before, the average value of retirement benefits in 401(k) plans declined by 33 percent.[72]

The security of millions of people was severely shaken, and many had to postpone retirement.

Even with the stock market rebound, the situation remains troubling. A 2013 Federal Reserve Survey of Consumer Finances found that, for working households nearing retirement, median combined 401(k)/IRA balances actually fell from $120,000 in 2010 to $111,000 in 2013. While younger households saw rising balances, retirement savings levels overall were clearly inadequate, and only about half of all households had any 401(k) assets at all.[73]

There are many problems within this system. For 401(k) plans to work at all well, individuals need to join them, contribute as much as possible, invest intelligently, and avoid withdrawing money, or using it as collateral for loans. Structures to ensure this are inadequate, and the 401(k)/IRA system plays a dual role—providing for retirement saving and supporting current consumption.

There are additional risks as well. In the shift from 401(k)s to IRAs, people are moving from a protected world— one with fee disclosure and fiduciary protections—to an unprotected one. While pensions offer steady and reliable monthly benefits, cashing out an IRA at retirement requires individual management of a big lump sum payment.

To supplement Social Security, depending on their income level, households are advised to get between one-quarter to one-half of their retirement income from retirement savings plans, such as 401(k)s. To produce this income, the typical household needs to save about 15 percent of earnings, which is well above today's actual saving rates. To make up for this deficit in savings would require younger households to save more and older households to work longer.[74]

As many as half of all private-sector workers have no employer-sponsored retirement plan, and are seriously at risk of not being able to maintain their standard of living once they retire. Several new programs at the federal and state level seek to expand the number of people who are saving via IRAs, both individually and through employers, but getting more people into this flawed system is a limited solution.

Not only are individual investors taking on all the risks of investing for retirement, they are doing so in an increasingly risky market environment. A troubling recent development has been the growth of actively managed funds, as compared to index funds. The fees charged for actively managed equity and bond funds are six times those of index funds, and many studies have shown them doing less well.[75]

While investment companies administering 401(k) plans must now disclose all the costs associated with administering the plans, significant problems remain. A January 2015 report from the Council of Economic Advisors indicated that an estimated $1.7 trillion of individual retirement account assets are invested in products that pay fees or commissions that pose conflicts of interest.

The current retirement system has been compared to the Wild West, full of lax and confusing rules and little enforcement. While "**investment** advisors" have a fiduciary duty under the Securities and Exchange Commission to act in the best interest of their clients, "**financial** advisors" — the term used by non-regulated insurance brokers, stockbrokers and mutual-fund firms — have no such obligation. Funds compete with each other by offering better deals to the brokers who invest them. The damage caused by advisers' conflict of interest, according to the Council of Economic Advisors, is a staggering $17 billion a year.[76]

We are all out gambling in the Wild West, and pension funds as well as individual retirement plans are struggling. Defined-benefit plans promise to pay benefits to retirees based on their salary and the length of time they worked. If plans run short of money, this not only affects the retirees, but creates a potential cost for whoever has to bail them out — often taxpayers.

The Federal Employees Retirement System (FERS) annuity supplements government workers' Social Security. FERS is in balance for current employees, thanks to hefty government contributions, but it is suffering from rising costs. The unfunded liability for employees still covered by the old civil service retirement system totals more than $630 billion. Since the recession, most states have been trimming pension costs for public-sector employees, but huge unfunded liabilities remain—as much as $800 billion. Defined benefit plans that are still managed by corporations have unfunded liabilities totaling around $355 billion, and recent legislation that allows companies to use higher return assumptions just pushes that problem further down the road.[77]

Hedge Funds—The Ultimate Gamble

The word "hedge" derives from the strategy of betting both directions, up and down. Hedging can be a necessary and quite normal business activity. For example, businesses with international operations use hedging strategies to insulate their operations from currency fluctuations.

Hedging becomes problematic when conducted in search of abnormal profits. Hedge funds are open only to professional investors with at least $1 million to bet. Results depend on the skill of the "stock-picker" to produce returns that surpass the overall market, so the fees are high. Until recently this high-stakes game was exempt from Security and Exchange Commission (SEC) reporting requirements. It was only with the Dodd-Frank Wall Street Consumer Protection Act in 2010 that U.S. hedge funds were required to register with the SEC.

There are some reports that hedge funds have been underperforming in recent years. According to a report released by Goldman Sachs in May 2013, hedge fund performance lagged behind the Standard & Poor's 500-stock index by approximately 10 percentage points that year, although most fund manager fees remain high.[78]

According to one study of hedge fund returns from 1998 to 2010, profits were consistently over-reported. Hedge fund managers earned an estimated $379 billion in fees during that time, while "real investors" earned only $70 billion in profits. Thus, 84 percent of the investment profits went to the managers, leaving only 16 percent for the investors. With the inclusion of the additional layer of fees associated with "fund of funds," through which about a third of hedge funds are purchased, industry fees go even higher, and the percentage left for investors drops.[79]

A rising number of institutional investors, including public and private pensions as well as university endowments and philanthropic foundations, are investing larger shares of their portfolios in hedge funds. Once considered an elite investment for wealthy individuals, a majority of hedge funds assets are now owned by institutional rather than private investors.

The lure of high returns on hedge funds has been hard to resist for pension fund managers in particular. The return-on-investment targets of seven to eight percent that are structured into pension plans are beyond the reach of the current low-interest-rate environment, and are creating an enormous challenge for pension fund managers. To redeem their promises to retiring teachers, firefighters and others, managers are risking more money with hedge funds in hope of yields higher than those on safer investments.

Unfunded liabilities in pension funds are just as onerous as other kinds of debt. Altogether, those unfunded pension liabilities add more than $2.5 trillion to America's $16 trillion Federal debt and $2.8 trillion state and local debt. Just as it is vital to reduce government deficits, it will eventually be necessary to bring down this pension funding deficit. One way would be to slash retirement benefits by 20 percent. Another would be to force employees to pay an additional 5 percent of their salaries toward such benefits. Or taxpayers could be forced to bail out pension funds as they get into trouble. Switching everyone over to defined-contribution plans, such as 401(k)s, would eventually solve the problem for young workers by shifting the risk to them. But that would still leave a huge unfunded liability for those approaching retirement and create future problems as individuals take on all the risk.[80]

Protecting our Institutional Health:
Threats and Opportunities

Although many of us had little individual relationship to Wall Street before the advent of 401(k)s, institutions that we were part of and that we counted on invested there. The endowments and savings of our Friends meetings, churches, and organizations; our schools, colleges and universities; and the service and philanthropic organizations that engage in the work to which we are committed — all have needed a place to be housed, and that house has overwhelmingly been the stock market.

The non-profit sector as a whole manages a lot of money. The roughly 1.5 million non-profits registered with the IRS in 2012 contributed about $887 billion to the U.S. economy — 5.4 percent of the country's gross domestic product.[81] Religious organizations received about a third of all private charitable contributions in 2009 — two and a half times the share of any other type of non-profit.[82] The country's 86,000 foundations held $715 billion in assets, and distributed a record $52 billion in 2012.[83]

Though the decisions about how the great majority of this money is invested are out of our hands, in the places where we do have leverage, there is compelling logic to apply the force at our command to those levers.

Even though most of these non-profit institutions, which lost so heavily in the Great Recession, have substantially recovered the value of their endowments, the question of institutional financial health has taken on a new urgency. Some big university endowments could actually be seen as part of the problem, because they have embraced the risky investment strategies that contributed to the stock market's collapse in 2008. Over the last 20 years, those flagship universities and many others moved away from traditional endowment holdings in domestic stocks and bonds, and placed more money into riskier asset classes, such as private equity, hedge funds, real estate, timberland, oil, and other commodities. Potential conflicts of interest have been identified among some college trustees who were affiliated with financial firms that managed endowment money.[84]

This trend has continued, with troubling implications. In an attempt to maintain long-term funding equity with their rivals, university endowment managers have shifted toward alternative investments, including hedge funds. At the other end of the higher education spectrum, state universities that used to rely mostly on public dollars are now scrambling to build endowments and are increasingly being led by CEOs with ties to the financial industry.

Savings and Debt

Unearned income and debt are two sides of the same coin. To the extent that we are unable to rely on savings enhanced by interest to fund future big ticket needs, we — or our children — face the prospect of going into debt and bearing the burden of having to pay that debt back with interest. People are going into more and more debt for a variety of reasons. They may simply have insufficient income to pay for basic needs. They may lack skills in financial management or future planning. They may be faced with expensive emergencies for which they lack adequate savings. They may have been manipulated by advertising and credit card industries to believe that they can buy more than they can afford. When we consider that almost all interest is paid by some form of debt, the continuing profitability of financial sector investments has to be mirrored by skyrocketing indebtedness, which we see today at all levels of society. While the issue of debt in general is a critical one, our focus here is on debt as it relates to savings, and we turn to the increasing challenges of affording higher education.

Financing Education

Besides saving for retirement, paying for college is the other way that many people become involved with compound interest — both as debtors and investors. To the extent that parents have insufficient savings to pay for college education, many students have little choice but to take on debt. This has become a major issue in the last several decades. What happened to bring us to this point?

65

In colonial times, the only higher education that existed was directed almost entirely toward religious study by wealthy white Protestant men. Classical liberal arts colleges followed. Then, in 1862, public agricultural and trade schools were authorized on federal land endowed to the states. In the early twentieth century, John Dewey argued that higher education promoted social progress and the greater good of the economy, but by 1940 only five percent of adults over 25 were college graduates.

The era of mass higher education began after World War II with the GI Bill, when nearly 4.4 million veterans returned home, set off for college, and the number of graduates tripled. In 1958, in response to Russia's launch of Sputnik, the National Defense Education Act established low interest government-backed student loans to encourage more students to pursue math and science degrees.[85]

The Higher Education Act of 1965, part of Johnson's Great Society, established Educational Opportunity Grants (later known as Pell Grants), encouraging colleges to aggressively pursue students with high financial need. The Guaranteed Student Loan Program (to become Stafford Loans) provided government loan subsidies to middle class students.

Between 1950 and 1970 the number of college graduates doubled again. In 1970, 68 percent of federal aid to college students was in the form of grants, and a Pell Grant could cover about two thirds of tuition at many universities. With baby boomers reaching college age, state appropriations to higher education increased more than fourfold from 1960 to 1975. In the late 1970s, however, a gap between the availability of federal aid and the cost of tuition began to appear and has been growing steadily ever since.[86]

Skyrocketing Tuition Costs
From 1978 to 2008, college tuition and fees rose at four times the cost of living, twice as much as medical cost inflation. Many reasons have been offered to explain this. A common one is that higher education lacks incentives to be cost efficient; on the contrary, universities must spend to make themselves as attractive as possible to their constituents. They spend on

facilities and faculties to attract the best and the brightest, on athletic and other programs to keep alumni support strong, on whatever will increase their ratings in external publications. With no drop in the supply of highly qualified applicants, this university "arms race" keeps ratcheting up the level of tuition.

Some people suggest that a major factor driving increasing costs is the expansion of university administration. Department of Education data show that between 1993 and 2009, administrative positions at colleges and universities grew at ten times the rate of growth of tenured faculty positions; as colleges are seen more as businesses, their CEO salaries have risen dramatically.[86]

Another factor has been the decreased role of public funding for higher education, starting with general spending cuts at the federal level in the Reagan years. In a gradual shift of responsibility for payment from government to students and their families, recent state budget cuts have prompted many public colleges to raise tuition and fees. State support for public colleges and universities has fallen by about 26 percent per full-time student since the early 1990s. In 2011, for the first time, public universities took in more revenue from tuition than from state funding. Enrolling 80 percent of U.S. college students, this can be seen as an effective privatization of public higher education.

The Role of Debt

With the decline of direct public spending on higher education, the emphasis has shifted increasingly to student loans. When the 1965 Higher Education Act first introduced the idea of government guaranteed loans, these loans were made by private bankers, with the government paying interest accrued while the student was in college, covering the difference between the low-interest rate and the market rate thereafter, and guaranteeing them in case of default.

In the 1980s and 1990s there was debate at the federal level about the role of private bankers in student debt. Liberals tended to favor the direct government loan system of the Eisenhower era, while conservatives viewed this as a government takeover. Not surprisingly, the bankers didn't want to lose out on such a lucrative market of guaranteed loans. A 1993 compromise phased in some direct federal loans while keeping guarantees in place for the bank loans. Aggressive marketing kept these loans more popular than the lesser-known government alternative.

It can be argued that the increase in federal student aid is another driver of increased tuition and fees. With more federal dollars available, universities can raise tuition or fees, confident that the federal loan subsidies will help cushion the increase for students. Thus, when Congress raises the loan limit so students can take out deeper loans, tuition is bid up to the new higher level that the student can now "afford" with loan subsidies. This is the same pattern we see in other domains, such as housing, where easy credit inflated the price of goods and services.

Recent changes in federal law strip students of the ability to declare bankruptcy, which also sends a message to lenders and colleges that the students are on the hook for any amount that they borrow — including late fees and interest — reducing the incentive to provide loans that can be reasonably paid back.

This situation helped spawn the growth of for-profit colleges, where enrollment increased 225 percent over the past two decades — and their stocks soared. According to a 2012 Department of Education report, for-profit colleges account for 10 percent of enrolled students but 44 percent of student loan defaults.[86]

Looking Forward

With the 2008 financial crisis, student bank loan money started drying up and the number of colleges turning to direct federal loans shot up. While banks lobbied hard to hang onto the lucrative government-backed student loan market, in 2010 Congress approved President Obama's plan for the government to take over the entire federal student loan program. In the process, interest rates have gone down, and there are more options for interest waivers and loan forgiveness. Ironically, however, the Department of Education is now responsible for both making loans that students may never be able to repay, and collecting on defaulted ones.

Many of the questions that have been raised in this discussion of the economics of higher education are beyond the scope of this book to fully examine. Clearly, however, the trajectory of expansion, both of increasing student debt and profligate university spending, is unsustainable in the long term. Particularly troubling is the timing. Throngs of first generation college goers, many from minority families, are embracing the promise of a college degree as their ticket to economic security, or at least the only route out of certain poverty. They are taking on more debt than students ever did in the past, at a time when the prospects of ever paying it back are increasingly dim. In the short term, this situation cries out for some form of loan forgiveness, or debt jubilee. Any long-term solution will have to involve, at minimum, removing the profit motive from education, some kind of institutional cost containment, and a mix of family and public financing that doesn't leave many college graduates, with little prospect for gainful employment, in virtual debt slavery. Individually, we don't want to wait to find new ways, outside of the traditional financial markets, to save for college.

Conclusion

People in this country are struggling to save as never before. More and more of the burden of providing for basic future needs is resting on the shoulders of individuals. For those who are able, it's hard to see any options other than playing the investment game as well as we can. Yet there are a surprising number of alternative, socially beneficial ways to use our savings that avoid some of the ethical dilemmas we create when we throw our lot in with an expansionary and profit-driven financial system. We will turn to these alternatives in the next chapter.

CHAPTER 7
Steps to Decrease Dependence on Speculative Financial Markets

We have seen how the profusion of IRAs and defined contribution pension plans has led more and more people of moderate means to be involved with the financial sector of the economy. Many of us are puzzled about how to do this with integrity. In this chapter, we will explore a variety of investment choices, from traditional stocks and bonds to socially responsible investing, and to alternatives such as direct public offerings, community investment, and peer-to-peer lending.

Most people with assets to invest choose publicly traded stocks and bonds. Some use a financial advisor to invest in publicly traded stocks and bonds of their own choosing. Many others buy shares in mutual funds, managed by financial professionals who invest in a diversified portfolio of stocks and bonds according to a variety of criteria. Mutual funds first became popular in the 1950s for those who wanted a higher return than a savings account provided, but did not want the responsibilities and risks of ownership. They are widely used today to save for retirement.

Socially Responsible Mutual Funds and Investment Advisors

For many years, conscientious people have tried to live out their religious and ethical values by channelling their savings into investments chosen not only for financial performance but also for the kinds of economic activities for which their savings are being used. Since the 1980s, this has been known as Socially Responsible Investing (SRI).

In the 1980s, mutual funds with SRI criteria, called "screens," began to be established. The early SRI funds had negative screens; they typically avoided buying stocks in businesses that make weapons, alcohol, or tobacco products. Then SRI funds began to be established with positive screens, to invest in companies that are ecologically sensitive, treat their workers well, and numerous other criteria, so that there are now many "screened" mutual funds to choose from, depending on an investor's values.

Most financial advisors are guided by the corporate ethic of "fiduciary responsibility," which quite simply is to make as much money as possible from the assets that are placed in their care. However, as SRI mutual funds gained increasing favor during the 1990s, SRI financial advisors began to help clients find investment opportunities that are consistent with their ethical standards, in addition to meeting their financial objectives.

Excluding fossil fuel companies from SRIs is relatively recent. The divestment movement, which has developed especially with strong support from 350.org (Go Fossil Free), has encouraged investors to shift investments away from fossil fuels.[87] Many organizations are supporting this call. The Shalom Center of Philadelphia, Pennsylvania, for example, calls its campaign "Move Our Money/Protect Our Planet (MOM/POP)," recalling deep religious traditions with the imagery of "Climate Plagues" and suggesting that individuals and institutions examine healing alternatives and ways to use money.[88] Fossil-fuel divestment is, of course, but one motive for removing personal investments from speculative financial markets.

Trying to be Fossil-Fuel Free

Much of my retirement savings is in TIAA-CREF, including the TIAA-CREF Social Choice Fund, which screens for alcohol, tobacco, and firearms, but not for fossil fuels. I am a "conservative investor" and prefer that my investments be managed by someone I trust. Our TIAA-CREF investment advisor suggested that I could convert the CREF portion to an IRA that could contain funds with the screens that I seek, and he sent a list of suggested funds, but when I researched the funds I realized that they didn't have the screens that I sought. (Some screen for companies that have under certain percentages of involvement with nuclear weapons, tobacco or firearms, gambling, abortion or the manufacture of contraceptives, pornography, land mines, child labor, and stem cell research. Some have general screens for positive environmental, social, and governance performances but nothing specifically eliminating for fossil fuel extraction.)

Inertia set in. We like TIAA-CREF and our advisor. I rationalize that the fossil fuel portion of my investments is small, and that I do communicate my concern that there is not a fossil fuel option to TIAA-CREF—verbally to my advisor, and in the TIAA-CREF online surveys.

Recently I discovered greenamerica.org, which has extremely helpful information, including a list of broad-based mutual funds that exclude fossil fuel companies by policy. The website also has information about banks that fund mountaintop removal coal mining, and provides a link to 350.org's list of the top 200 fossil fuel companies.

I have communicated with our TIAA-CREF advisor to inquire whether the funds listed in greenamerica.org are available to me in an IRA through TIAA-CREF. If they are not available, it will be time for me to decide whether to overcome my inertia. I don't want to switch advisors and would prefer to remain with TIAA-CREF, but it is important to me that my retirement funds do not profit from harm to the planet.

—Deb Foote Faulkner

Friends Fiduciary Corporation

Founded in 1898, the Friends Fiduciary Corporation (FFC) is a not-for-profit corporation providing socially responsible investment management services to 320 Quaker meetings, churches, schools and organizations across the country. FFC manages over $325 million, following an investment philosophy guided by Quaker principles:

> "Quaker testimonies and values guide FFC's investment activities in three primary ways: we actively screen out companies that do not meet our Quaker values investing criteria; we engage in shareholder advocacy by dialoging directly with companies, filing shareholder proposals and voting our proxies, consistent with Quaker values on environmental, social and governance issues; and we share our unique, and under-represented Quaker business perspective on important policy issues." [89]

Beginning in 2011, several Monthly Meetings in Philadelphia Yearly Meeting formally asked FFC to divest from companies profiting from the fossil fuel industry. In 2012, the Yearly Meeting's Eco-Justice Working Group began to connect and strengthen those voices in support of our testimony on integrity and 350.org's fossil fuel divestment campaign.

In 2013, FFC decided, without fanfare, to eliminate coal companies and related utilities from their investments, and also to dispose of their "big oil" stock. At the same time, Friends Fiduciary began offering an alternative Quaker Green Fund, with no holdings in the 200 largest companies associated with fossil fuels, and 12 percent of their holdings in companies that are helping to advance a low-carbon energy future. At present they feel unable to commit more of their assets to such alternative investments. [90]

In response to this good news, the Working Group's attention shifted to encouraging Quaker meetings to switch their investments to the Green Fund, even though the anticipated returns would be somewhat lower. By the middle of 2015, at least 15 of FFC's investors had moved a total of $15.3 million to the Green Fund.

Quakers Divest from Hewlett-Packard and Veolia Environment

Friends Fiduciary Corporation has dropped its holdings in Hewlett-Packard and Veolia Environment. The two multinational corporations are the focus of a global divestment and boycott movement that charges them with supporting Israel's 45-year-old military occupation of the Palestinian territories.

"Hewlett-Packard was removed from Friends Fiduciary's investments because it provides IT consulting services to the Israeli Navy," said Jeffery W. Perkins, the Executive Director of Friends Fiduciary. Veolia Environment, the world's largest water privatization company, was removed because of "environmental and social concerns." Veolia provides segregated water and transportation services to Israeli settlers living illegally in the occupied Palestinian territories.[91]

In April 2012, Friends Fiduciary was also the first investment firm in the U.S. to remove Caterpillar Corporation from its list of socially responsible corporations. According to Anne Remley,

> "We Ann Arbor Quakers asked the Friends Fiduciary Corporation to divest from these companies because we don't want to support corporations whose products are used in gross human rights violations carried out by the Israeli military in its occupation of the Palestinian territories. Hewlett-Packard makes products used by the Israeli navy, which enforces the illegal blockade of Gaza. Caterpillar bulldozers are weaponized and used to destroy Palestinian homes and agricultural land, and to build illegal, Jewish-only settlements on occupied Palestinian land. And Veolia builds transportation systems used to transport Jewish settlers between those settlements and Israel. We're pleased that the Friends Fiduciary Corporation is no longer involved with these endeavors." [91]

The action of Friends Fiduciary in dropping these three firms marks a significant breakthrough in the global campaign to hold corporations accountable for supporting Israel's human rights and international law violations in the Palestinian territories.

Stock Markets

While stock exchanges originally provided a public service by allowing companies to raise money from a large number of investors by selling shares of ownership, today capital formation is a small part of what happens in stock markets. According to John Fullerton, former managing director at JP Morgan and founder of the Capital Institute, an organization dedicated to making capital markets more sustainable and socially beneficial,

"Today's stock markets are primarily about speculating on the future prices of stock certificates; they are largely disconnected from real investment or what goes on in the real economy of goods and services... recent history has shown that our world leading liquid markets are as well the source of extreme global instability with dire and ongoing consequences."[92]

Fullerton cites a variety of reasons why stock markets are no longer as beneficial to society as originally envisioned:

- The privatization of stock exchanges, destroying their public purpose mandate and instead making the growth of trading volume their single-minded goal and high-frequency traders their preferred customers;
- The unrestrained technology arms race in computing power combined with the adoption of technology-driven information flow spurring the rapid acceleration of trading volume, which at critical times can be highly destabilizing;
- The misguided ascent of "shareholder wealth maximization" (at the expense of all other stakeholder interests) in our business schools, board rooms, and the corporate finance departments on Wall Street;
- The well-intended but equally misguided practice of using stock-based incentives, and stock options in particular, as the dominant form of senior management compensation, which incentivizes them to focus only on short-term results at the expense of the long-term health of the enterprise, people and planet;
- The misalignment of interests between short-term focused Wall Street intermediaries and real investors such as pension funds whose timeframe should be measured in decades;

- Regulators' lack of courage and confidence to counter the trader-driven paradigm and institute substantive structural reform such as a Financial Transactions Tax and other reforms that would penalize excessive speculation while incentivizing long-term productive investment.[92]

Some may be surprised to learn that buying stock in a corporation brings few real benefits to that company. After the Initial Public Offering (IPO) when a corporation first sells shares, subsequent buying and selling of shares provides no additional money to the firm other than through secondary offerings that are rarely used, as they dilute the value of the stock. Minimally, investments contribute to a higher stock price, but the benefits to a corporation from this increased price are relatively small—mostly easier access to credit and protection from being "taken over." As Fullerton points out, those most interested in high stock prices are CEOs and management who increasingly receive stock options as part of their salaries.

Shareholder Activism

One way faith communities have become more active in influencing corporations' actions is through shareholder activism: foundations, endowments, and individuals buy stock—often at the minimum number of shares—in a corporation not to profit from its dividends, but with the goal of influencing the corporation through shareholder resolutions or proposals. Many religious organizations are members of the Interfaith Center for Corporate Responsibility (ICCR), which offers shareholder proposals to compel management to take an action in a variety of areas from executive compensation to implementing greener processes or improving working conditions. At corporations' annual meetings of shareholders, these proposals are considered and voted upon by all shareholders.

Alternative Forms of Investment

It is possible, though not easy, to make ethical choices about purchasing stocks and bonds. It is much easier to move assets from unscreened to screened mutual funds, or from funds with weaker screens to those with stronger ones. SRI financial

Fadvisors can help identify these kinds of opportunities in financial markets and among mutual funds. Yet some people would prefer to invest outside of these markets altogether.

As new economy writer Keith Harrington explains we need to move toward more "patient" methods of financing or favor the creation and development of stable businesses providing concrete societal and ecological benefits.

"If you want to build a mere façade of prosperity, a house of cards, then fast money is the way to go. But an economy that's built to last and built for all requires the time and care that's only possible with a patient financial system."[93]

Harrington describes the benefits that investors reap through participating in the patient economy:

"It's mostly the knowledge that they're building real businesses dedicated to growing community wealth and to promoting other new-economy values such as workplace democracy. By putting limits on investor privilege and curbing the speculator profit motive, patient finance reorients the purpose of investment toward actually developing the long-term viability of enterprise, so that it becomes a source of prosperity for all stakeholders – not just shareholders."[93]

There have always been ways of using savings to benefit local people and businesses. But since the 1980s, when savings institutions became absorbed into the larger financial system, these ways have been far less known or available to most people. Yet with the advent of new technologies, a host of alternative forms of investment are now emerging that can provide financial returns while more directly benefitting society.

Most of these alternatives have lower rates of return and greater risk, but are more socially beneficial. Every investor needs to balance personal priorities and shift investments accordingly. Not every step will be right for every person. Steps that are not right for someone today may be right for the same person at some time in the future.

People who are looking for other opportunities to invest may consider new avenues that more concretely support the birthing of a new economy. The vision of this new economy is one that is more democratic, equitable, and environmentally sustainable.

Investing outside of Wall Street

During the Occupy movement in 2011, I felt conflicted that I had my retirement money largely in the stock market. My broker is a good friend of my brother's and I had stayed with him out of loyalty to the two of them. I was always uncomfortable, always asking for socially responsible investments…often refusing to invest in certain companies, but still complicit in an unjust economy. So, I called my broker and told him to sell everything. I wanted out of Wall Street. He was shocked, but complied.

By then, I had invested in some alternatives such as solar panels on my roof sufficient to cover most of my electric needs, paying off my house, and moving my checking and money market account to a local bank, but I was clear I had to do more. Since then, I have found several uses for my savings with which I feel more comfortable.

1. I made a sizeable loan to my local food co-op to help finance its expansion into my neighborhood.
2. After hearing about the opportunity through a friend who knew the owner, I made a large investment in a biogas project in Ohio. Their new plant takes organic waste from firms including Campbell's Soup, Purina, and others and uses an anaerobic digestion process to convert it into methane that can be used as power.
3. I provided a mortgage to some relatives to purchase a camp in the Adirondacks. They were unable to get a mortgage from a bank, so we created one through a lawyer and they are paying me interest—much less than they would have had to pay to a bank.
4. I also give away as much money as possible to charitable organizations, spurred by my generous former employer, which matches anything I give at $2 for each $1 of mine.
5. I have recently learned of a friend who used her inheritance to purchase a rental property that she rents out at below market rate (but still making a better interest rate than if invested in the stock market) to a dear friend, who was unable to afford a home of her own. I am considering making such an investment myself if I can find something suitable in this area.

—*Hollister Knowlton*

Endowments and an Organization's Mission

During a discussion with missionary groups about investing, Theologian Ched Myers made an interesting point about a paradox of many social justice organizations and how they use their substantial monetary resources. Many larger groups have established multi-million dollar endowments, which they invest in stocks and bonds so as to use the dividends to partially fund their operations. He gave the example of a fictitious organization that has an annual budget of $5 million and an endowment of $45 million. The paradox he pointed to is that the organization has direct control over $50 million, but places only 10 percent of that money directly to work toward efforts related to its mission. Ninety-five percent of its money ($45 million) is instead fed into the bloated financial sector with minimal societal benefit. Imagine, he asked, if they were to place 100 percent, or even 50 percent, of their endowment was invested in places like the alternatives described here. They would receive lower returns, but have a larger societal impact and more of their money would be going toward supporting efforts better aligned with their social mission, be that through community development organizations, sustainable agriculture farms, alternative energy projects, or to helping free the poor from debt.

The Oblate International Pastoral Investment Trust, which helps fund the activities of the Missionary Oblates of Mary Immaculate around the world, recently shifted seven million dollars of its trust into FIRST Brazil Impact Investing Fund that helps finance a variety of companies that provide services and products to low-income families. The shift is part of the more than $35 million that the trust has moved into community development investing. Friar Seamus Finn, the trust's director explains that this type of investing "suits and fits better with our desire to be constructive and look for positive impact investments."[94]

Patricia Kind Family Foundation

One example of a foundation responsibly using more of its savings to support mission-oriented activities is shown by Laura Kind McKenna, managing trustee of the Patricia Kind Family Foundation. McKenna evaluates social impact first and foremost, and the potential financial return is secondary.

McKenna's advice: Do not touch the five percent you are legally obligated to grant. Instead, pull another five percent from your corpus (the 95 percent of assets that remain after grants are deployed). With that five percent, make a zero- or low-interest loan or a private equity investment in a social enterprise that aligns with your mission.

An example: In 2012, the Patricia Kind Foundation made a multi-year, zero-interest $37,000 loan towards Depaul House USA, a national transitional housing nonprofit for the homeless with a branch in Germantown, Pennsylvania. The loan, structured to demand increasing repayments over the course of its 10-year lifespan, helped Depaul launch Immaculate Cleaning Services (ICS), a for-profit business that employs Depaul residents.

Three years later, ICS has already paid back nearly three-fifths of their loan. After paying their employees and paying back their loans, ICS is now generating a little under $1,000 in unrestricted funds for Depaul every month.

The most detrimental failure a foundation can make, McKenna believes, is choosing to remain inactive with their corpus. Her advice for colleagues looking to join her? Stop vetting vehicles through financial institutions. "When people say there aren't enough opportunities out there, they're only looking at opportunities through financial institutions," she said. "Look at mission first. Take a risk with a social entrepreneur."[95]

Direct Public Offerings

Many small and medium-sized businesses have a difficult time raising money, as they are too small to attract large investors, yet too big for other sources such as family and friends. The Small Business Administration (SBA) estimates that the aggregate amount needed by businesses seeking between $250,000 and $5 million to be $60 billion. The problem is so common that the SBA created a term to describe it: "capital chasm." Increasingly, these businesses are using the Internet to sell shares of ownership directly to investors without the aid of an investment bank or a broker who charges massive fees and is rarely interested in financing smaller enterprises.

For investors, a Direct Public Offering (DPO) means that more of their investment goes directly to the business instead of being siphoned off by an investment bank. As they are buying public shares, they can pull out of the investment at any time by selling their shares. *Cutting Edge Capital* lists a number of entities that facilitate direct public offerings.[96]

The Security Exchange Commission recently made important changes in investment rules that will facilitate DPOs. First-time start-up companies are now allowed to raise up to $1 million online from non-accredited investors. Previously, only accredited investors could invest in private deals. "For the first time, ordinary Americans will be able to go online and invest in entrepreneurs that they believe in," explained President Barack Obama as he signed the JOBS Act into law in 2012.[97]

As start-ups are highly risky, non-accredited investors are limited to investing a maximum of five percent of their income or ten percent of their net worth in DPOs.

Evergreen Direct Investment Method

John Fullerton notes that conscientious investors in the responsible investing movement

"seeking to embed environmental, social and governance values (ESG) into their investment decision-making are hamstrung by the investment method chosen. Specifically, trying to apply ESG to

what is inherently a speculative stock valuations game often feels like pushing on a string. Without conscious awareness, we have confused speculation for investment."[98]

The Capital Institute proposes the Evergreen Direct Investment Method in which institutional investors like foundations and pension funds can build long-term relationships with enterprises that express their values and "can achieve attractive and resilient long-term financial returns that match their liabilities, while directly embedding ESG values into negotiated investment partnerships." The method envisions, "stewardship-minded investors negotiating direct relationships with corporate management with an explicit requirement to build long-term environmental, social and governance values and parameters into the enterprise capital investment process, even if it entails some short-term negative consequences." The advantage is that investors can have a real say in the actions of a company while providing "stable cash flows of mature, slow- or no-growth business enterprises that the valuations-game-driven speculators leave on the trash heap."[98]

Slow Money

Slow Money is a movement that aims to "bring money back down to Earth" by helping investors to "invest as if food, farms and fertility mattered." They do this by connecting investors to small food enterprises throughout the U.S. From farm cooperatives to urban agriculture enterprises to manure farms and more, Slow Money has helped funnel over $40 million into more than 400 small farm efforts around the country.[99]

Community and Faith-based Development Investing

Another alternative to investing in the financial markets is to invest in community and faith-based development organizations that support local efforts to provide affordable housing, jobs and economic development, especially in low-income communities. This is sometimes referred to as "impact" or "mission-related" investing.

Some examples include the Mennonite Church USA's stewardship agency called "Everence," which provides financial products and services that are aligned with their founding values. They have developed two programs for community investing: mPower, which provides funding for international microfinance organizations; and nSpire, which supports faith-based community development projects throughout the United States.[100]

Quakers in New Zealand have created the "Quaker Investment Ethical Trust," which provides low-interest loans to individuals and for community development, while providing stable returns for investors.[101]

The World Council of Churches established "Oikocredit" in 1968 to provide an ethical investment channel for churches and related organizations to provide credit to enterprises that support the disadvantaged. It invests in microfinance, fair trade organizations and agricultural enterprises around the world, especially Asia and Latin America.[102]

"Kiva" is a similar organization that channels investors' money to microlenders around the world. The loans that individuals make are interest free, so the reward comes in an increased sense of solidarity rather than monetary return.[103]

Peer-to-peer Financing

The original propose of peer-to-peer (P2P) financing was to democratize finance by using Internet platforms to directly match people in need of a loan with those with money to lend and looking for higher returns than other investments. By cutting out banks as intermediaries, the platforms are able to provide lower interest rates for borrowers and higher returns for lenders, while disrupting the oligopoly of a shrinking number of financial institutions.

Yet, we see that large financial institutions are coming to dominate peer-to-peer markets as well. According to *The Economist*, "[i]n America [sic], the two largest P2P lenders, Lending Club and Prosper, have 98 percent of the market"[104] and an increasing amount of the money loaned on these platforms comes not from individual lenders but from hedge funds and large banks, "Only a third of the money coming to Lending Club is now from retail investors."[104]

In her aptly titled article, "Wall Street is hogging the peer-to-peer lending market," financial reporter Shelly Banjo refers to a study by Orchard Platform:

> "[A]ll of the loans made by Lending Club and Prosper in 2008 were fractional, meaning individual lenders came together and each put in as little as $25 toward a loan. Now, only 35 percent of the loan dollars are coming from fractional loans. In 2014, the other 65 percent of the more than $3 billion loans on the two platforms came from investors snatching up whole loans, which are almost always made by institutional investors rather than individuals."[105]

Some market analysts say that large institutions are necessary to scale up to provide needed capital, but the reality today is that "investor demand is now outstripping the loan supply, spurring fierce competition among investors to snatch the best loans first," according to Amy Cortese writing in the *New York Times*. Orchard Platform has shown that these investors are now snapping up nearly 50 percent of whole loans on Prosper in less than 10 seconds. They manage this by using complicated computer algorithms similar to those used by high-speed traders in other capital markets. These algorithm-armed investors end up scooping up the highest quality loans (the ones most likely to be paid back) leaving the poorest quality loans for everyday investors whom P2P lending is supposed to benefit.[106]

While the larger P2P lending platforms have been bought out by the same banks and hedge funds that peer lending was supposed to replace, at least one large-scale platform has maintained fidelity to the idea of individuals helping other individuals: Zopa, the world's first peer-to-peer lending platform and currently the United Kingdom's largest. Since its inception in February 2005, Zopa has facilitated more than $1 billion in loans, all between individuals, showing that institutional money is not necessary to scale up a P2P lending platform.[107]

While few of the larger P2P platforms remain purely peer-to-peer, there are a number of other ways to invest savings without becoming part of the overgrown financial system.

Church P2P Lending

Some churches are helping their members dig themselves out of debt through low-interest loans. The United Methodist Church created the Jubilee Assistance Fund especially to help people unable to pay the exorbitant interest rates of payday lenders and others who take advantage of people with low incomes. By providing much lower interest loans, churches help their members avoid evictions, bankruptcies, and other financial woes.

Lending Circles

For millennia people without access to large amounts of capital have created mechanisms within their communities to provide pools of money for investing. One of the most common methods is lending circles, in which friends and family agree to contribute a fixed amount of money into a common pool that is given to one member of the group each week. For example, ten friends agree to give $100 every two weeks to the organizer. At the end of each month, the $2000 is given to one member of the group. The circle continues until each member receives at least once. A variety of online platforms now exist that help people find nearby lending circles and help groups to organize the process.

Conclusion

While the options described in this chapter are useful for those who have surplus income after paying bills and are able to create long-term savings, they leave out millions of people who live paycheck to paycheck. As a society, we need to find ways to provide economic security to those with lower incomes as well, possibilities we explore in the next chapter.

CHAPTER 8

Big Picture Ways of
Rethinking Income Security

In traditional agrarian societies, old people count on their families. This is probably the oldest, and likely still the most common, form of retirement security. Extended families acknowledge a bond of mutual obligation with the old people in their midst, and care for them when they are no longer able to care for themselves. In contemporary modern societies, family bonds and obligations still exist, but the security that they provide is limited by geographical distances, but significantly augmented by the work of social organizations and government programs. After first describing the historical origins of organized social care, this chapter discusses two modern forms of income security. The first is the Social Security system, as begun in the 1930s and expanded in the 1960s. The second is a guaranteed annual income, as envisioned in President Roosevelt's economic bill of rights, proposed by President Nixon and approved by the U.S. House of Representatives in 1970, but failed in the Senate. It has been practiced by smaller jurisdictions in the U.S. and Canada.

Roots of Social Insurance
for our Most Vulnerable Citizens

The English Poor Law of 1601 was an early acknowledgement of the state's responsibility to provide for the welfare of its citizens. Taxes were raised to run relief activities for the "deserving" poor. These services, mostly poorhouses, were intentionally made as unpleasant as possible, to discourage free-loading and dependency.[108]

Other early systems were based on traditional care of family members and social organizations. The craft guilds of the Middle Ages supported groups of artisans in their work life, provided financial support in times of need, and helped pay funeral expenses. "Friendly societies" were more general mutual associations for insurance, pensions or savings, and the forerunners of the fraternal organizations such as Freemasons, the Fraternal Order of Eagles, Elks, the Knights of Columbus, etc. Many of these fraternal organizations originated in Europe and were transplanted to the colonies. Others were established on American soil.

While each fraternal organization had its distinctive elements, a member of one group summed up the common theme of mutual support well: "to establish a system for the care of the widows and orphans, the aged and disabled, and enable every worthy member to protect himself from the ills of life and make substantial provision through cooperation with our members, for those who are nearest and dearest."[109]

These fraternal organizations were widespread in the United States. A conservative estimate is that one-third of adult American males belonged to lodges in 1910, and they sponsored a wide variety of social services, including orphanages, hospitals, job exchanges, homes for the elderly, and scholarship programs.

At the same time that mutual societies such as these were expanding, the state was beginning to claim responsibility for its poor. The system of local taxation to help the worthy destitute was brought to the colonies, and for much of the 18th and 19th centuries most poverty relief was provided in the almshouses and poorhouses, with other charities playing a small additional role.

The aftermath of the Civil War brought a new sense of public responsibility for the less fortunate. Disabled soldiers and survivors of deceased breadwinners constituted a larger group of demonstrably "deserving" poor than the country had ever known. In response, the nation's first full-fledged pension system, for Civil War veterans, was instituted. In 1894 military pensions accounted for 37 percent of the entire federal budget, and by 1910, over 90 percent of the remaining Civil War veterans were receiving benefits, although nothing went to survivors of the Confederate side.[110]

Nor did this lead to an expanded view on rights to retirement benefits in general. Most older workers continued to be simply dismissed when their productive years were behind them. While a few companies pioneered pension plans for industrial workers in the late 1800s, by 1932 only about 15 percent of the labor force had any kind of potential employment-related pension, and barely five percent of the elderly were receiving retirement pensions.

Demographic changes were making the traditional systems of economic security increasingly unworkable. With growing industrialism, economic security was becoming increasingly out of individual control. Willingness to work hard did not necessarily translate into a job or a living wage. A marked increase in life expectancy, due to public health and sanitation improvements, combined with urbanization and the stresses on the extended family was turning us into a country that was older, more urban and with fewer of its people nested in a larger family context.

Impact of the Great Depression

The Great Depression was devastating to the elderly in the United States, with the best estimates indicating that in 1934 over half lacked sufficient income to be self-supporting.

A spurt of state pension legislation followed the Crash, so that by 1935 thirty states had some form of old-age pension program for the destitute. However, only about three percent of the elderly were actually receiving benefits under these state plans, and the average amount was about 65 cents a day.

With precipitous declines in the stock market, corporate wealth, investment, GNP, employment, and wages came radical calls to action. Louisiana Governor Huey Long's populist "Share Our Wealth" plan called upon the federal government to guarantee every family in the nation an annual income of $2,000 (enough in 1934 for a home, radio, automobile, and ordinary conveniences), along with old age pensions for everyone over 60, and limiting private fortunes to $50 million, legacies to $5 million, and annual incomes to $1 million.[111]

There was little appetite at the federal level for such radical plans. Soon after the Crash some wanted to sit tight and hope for a turnaround. When it became clear that more was needed, others, like President Hoover, hoped in vain that the model of volunteer public/private reconstruction that happened in Europe after World War I could be repeated. A third group called for expanding welfare benefits for those hardest hit by the Depression, beyond the clearly inadequate state systems.

Roosevelt and the Beginnings of Social Security

With President Roosevelt's election in 1932, the debate changed. His economic security proposal was different, based on social insurance rather than welfare assistance. This was not a new idea; it was familiar across the Atlantic as an expression of European social welfare tradition, but it opened up fresh possibilities at home.

The two basic features of social insurance are: the principle under which a group of persons are "insured" in some way against a defined risk, like the unemployment of old age. That insurance is shaped in part by broader social objectives, rather than solely by the self-interest of the individual participants.

Social insurance, as articulated by Roosevelt, would address the permanent problem of economic insecurity for the elderly by creating a work-related, contributory system in which workers would provide for their own future economic security through taxes paid while employed. This was an alternative both to reliance on welfare and to radical changes in our capitalist system. In the context of its time, it can be seen as a moderately conservative, yet activist, response to the challenges of the Depression.

On June 8, 1934, Roosevelt, in a message to the Congress, announced his intention to provide a program for Social Security:

> "Security was attained in the earlier days through the interdependence of members of families upon each other and of the families within a small community upon each other. The complexities of great communities and of organized industry make less real these simple means of security. Therefore, we are compelled to employ the active interest of the Nation as a whole through government to encourage a greater security for each individual who composes it . . . This seeking for a greater measure of welfare and happiness does not indicate a change in values. It is rather a return to values lost in the course of our economic development and expansion . . ."[112]

The Social Security Act was signed by President Roosevelt on August 14, 1935. In addition to the program we now think of as Social Security, it included unemployment insurance, old-age assistance, aid to dependent children, and grants to the states to provide various forms of medical care.[113]

Expansion of Social Security since 1965

While there were many changes over the next thirty years, including a shift from individual to family benefits and the addition of benefits for disability, the most significant was the Medicare bill, signed by President Lyndon Johnson on July 30, 1965. With the signing of this bill, the Social Security Administration became responsible for administering a new social insurance program that extended health coverage to almost all Americans aged 65 or older. Johnson had this to say:

> "Thirty years ago, the American people made a basic decision that the later years of life should not be years of despondency and drift. The result was enactment of our Social Security program. . . . Since World War II, there has been increasing awareness of the fact that the full value of Social Security would not be realized unless provision were made to deal with the problem of costs of illnesses among our older citizens. . . . Compassion and reason dictate that this logical extension of our proven Social Security system will supply the prudent, feasible, and dignified way to free the aged from the fear of financial hardship in the event of illness."[114]

Nearly 20 million beneficiaries enrolled in Medicare in the first three years of the program.

In the Social Security Amendments of 1972, Congress federalized the "other needy adult categories" that had been carried by states, creating the Supplemental Security Income program (SSI) and assigning responsibility for it to SSA. These amendments also legislated a regular increase in benefits based on the cost of living allowance (COLA).[115]

"Welfare reform" of 1996 put term limits and work requirements on some SSI recipients, and terminated access for most non-citizens. Legislation in 2000 allowed those who were still working to access Social Security benefits, and a 2003 law provided for a voluntary prescription drug benefit under the Medicare program—the largest single expansion of the Medicare system since its creation in 1965.

More than 90 percent of all workers are now in jobs covered by Social Security. From 220,000 people receiving monthly Social Security benefits in 1940, that number has grown to 50 million today, one in seven U.S. citizens. Social Security has become an essential facet of modern life, and a foundation of our retirement security system.

Yet Social Security has not solved the problem of income insecurity. While it provides a financial floor for old age, most of those who try to live on it with no other assets are living in poverty. Furthermore, it is questionable how much more the model can be expanded. With numbers of retirees growing in relation to numbers in the workforce, how much more can the current generation of workers forego in present wages to pay for the retirement needs of their elders? Do we need to look more widely for models of government social insurance?

Guaranteed Minimum Income for All
Roots of the idea of economic rights. In his State of the Union address in January 1944, President Roosevelt said,

"We have come to a clear realization of the fact that true individual freedom cannot exist without economic security and independence. 'Necessitous men are not free men.' People who are hungry and out of a job are the stuff of which dictatorships are made.

91

"In our day these economic truths have become accepted as self-evident. We have accepted, so to speak, a second Bill of Rights under which a new basis of security and prosperity can be established for all regardless of station, race, or creed.

"Among these are:

"the right to a useful and remunerative job in the industries or shops or farms or mines of the Nation;

"the right to earn enough to provide adequate food and clothing and recreation;

"the right of every farmer to raise and sell his products at a return which will give him and his family a decent living;

"the right of every businessman, large and small, to trade in an atmosphere of freedom from unfair competition and domination by monopolies at home or abroad;

"the right of every family to a decent home;

"the right to adequate medical care and the opportunity to achieve and enjoy good health; and

"the right to adequate protection from the economic fears of old age, sickness, accident, and unemployment; the right to a good education. ...

"America's own rightful place in the world depends in large part upon how fully these and similar rights have been carried into practice for our citizens. For unless there is security here at home there cannot be lasting peace in the world."[116]

Roosevelt was certainly not the first to be concerned about the provision of income security. Revolutionary War figure Thomas Paine called for the establishment of a public system of economic security for the new nation.[117] He proposed a system whereby those inheriting property would pay a 10 percent inheritance tax to create a special fund out of which a one-time stipend of 15 pounds sterling would be paid to each citizen upon attaining age 21, to give them a start in life, and annual benefits of 10 pounds sterling to be paid to every person age 50 and older, to guard against poverty in old-age.[118]

Various progressive income maintenance programs were proposed during the Great Depression, but were eclipsed by Roosevelt's more moderate Social Security Act. Starting in the 1940s, an economist at the other end of the political spectrum,

Milton Friedman, proposed a "negative income tax." In this model, a government subsidy would be triggered when household's income dipped below a specified floor, with the amount designed to raise the household's income to that minimum level.[119]

Guaranteed annual income and President Nixon. A guaranteed income came closest to becoming political reality in this country in 1970 under the leadership of Republican President Richard Nixon. The House passed a bill by a vote of 243 to 155 establishing the principle that the Government should guarantee every family a minimum annual income.[120]

What were the factors that allowed the idea of a Guaranteed Annual Income (GAI) to be a bi-partisan possibility in the late 1960s? There was the "rediscovery" of poverty in the United States — inspired in part by Michael Harrington's book, *The Other America*.[121] President Lyndon Johnson started his War on Poverty. Martin Luther King declared in 1967 that "the solution to poverty is to abolish it directly by a now widely discussed measure: the guaranteed income."[122]

In 1969 a presidential commission recommended in its report, *Poverty Amid Plenty: The American Paradox* that because poverty was caused by forces beyond an individual's control rather than by personal failing, the problem must be dealt with by the government. Over 1,000 university economists signed a letter supporting a GAI a year earlier, and a similar proposal was also floated by a panel of business leaders appointed by New York Governor Nelson Rockefeller.

No one liked the existent welfare policies. Liberals saw them as demeaning and inadequate, while conservatives disliked the bureaucracy, the specter of creating a dependent class, and the perceived threat to two-parent families. There was also a widespread belief that the war on poverty could be won. All of these factors helped to move GAI into the mainstream.

President Nixon championed a program that would benefit

"the working poor, as well as the nonworking; families with dependent children headed by a father, as well as those headed by a mother...

"What I am proposing is that the Federal Government build a foundation under the income of every American family with dependent children that cannot care for itself."[123]

For a family of four without any other income, Nixon's plan would provide $1,600 ($10,121 in 2013 dollars). But a family with income from employment would get declining support until that income reached $3,920 ($24,798 in 2013 dollars). Ultimately, the vast majority of benefits would have gone to the "working poor," a significant departure from then-existing programs that denied welfare benefits to those who were employed.

The fate of Nixon's Family Assistance Plan (FAP) may be instructive as we grapple with this issue of government income maintenance. Conservatives thought the proposal too generous, and liberal politicians and welfare rights activists thought the benefits too stingy. Liberals opposed the work requirements inherent in FAP, the very feature of the program that conservatives found most appealing. The Labor Department saw it as a threat to the minimum wage. So the plan stalled in the Senate and, after several more unsuccessful tries, Nixon finally gave it up.

Prospects for a guaranteed annual income. Times have changed. That was an era when people believed that government was an appropriate entity to address social problems. The influence of the New Deal era could still be felt, in the idea that full citizenship entails not only political and civic rights but also economic rights. There was discourse about what obligations people have to one another, as compared to now, when public welfare is seen more and more as subordinate to unstoppable market forces. Public discourse now includes the idea that in giving benefits to the poor, the government is interfering with the "market signals" that are telling them to work, thus making work and self-sufficiency less attractive than welfare.

Yet, the idea of a guaranteed income has been gaining traction again in recent years, on both the left and the right. Conservatives like the potential for efficiency and shrinking federal bureaucracy by eliminating dozens of "means-tested" programs. It embodies a conservative vision that sees public policy not as the manager of society but as an enabler of bottom-up incremental improvements. A basic income might be enough to live on, but not enough to live very well on. Such a program would be designed to end abject poverty without encouraging sloth or dependency.

Liberals like the prospect of lifting millions out of poverty. It would certainly be attractive to recipients. Creating a single point of access would make the lives of those who are struggling financially easier. If they knew they had something to fall back on, workers could negotiate better wages and conditions, or go back to school, or quit a low-paying job to care for a child or aging relative. And with an unconditional basic income, workers wouldn't have to worry about how making more money might lead to the loss of crucial benefits. A guaranteed income could also help society in general adjust to the disappearance of low-skill, low-wage jobs.[124]

It turns out that there is not just speculation about results, but also hard evidence. In the mid-1970s, the tiny Canadian town of Dauphin in Manitoba tried an experiment in social policy called "Mincome." For a short period of time, all the residents of the town received a guaranteed minimum income. About 1,000 poor families got monthly checks to supplement their earnings. Evelyn Forget, a health economist at the University of Manitoba, has done extensive research on the results. Some of her findings were expected: poverty disappeared. But others were more surprising: high-school completion rates went up; hospitalization rates went down. "If you have a social program like this, community values themselves start to change," Forget said.[125]

A guaranteed annual income would not be cheap. In 2012, there were 179 million Americans between the ages of 21 and 65 (when Social Security would kick in). The poverty line was $11,945. Thus, giving each working-age American a basic income equal to the poverty line would cost $2.14 trillion. Cutting all federal and state benefits for low-income Americans would save around a trillion dollars per year, so there would still be a significant gap that would have to be closed by revenue increases, such as higher taxes or closing existing loopholes.[126]

The arguments for a guaranteed annual income may be growing. Wages are stagnant and unemployment is high, both in Europe and at home. The Swiss are already in motion, having gathered enough signatures — 126,000 — for a national referendum on providing a monthly income to every citizen.[127]

Despite record corporate earnings and skyrocketing fortunes for the already well-off, the job market is simply not rewarding many fully employed workers with a decent way of life. Millions of households have had no real increase in earnings since the late 1980s, and more and more people's full time earnings do not add up to a living wage.[128]

The United States already has experience with a variation of basic income. Alaska's Permanent Fund Dividend, which distributes a portion of oil production royalties to every Alaskan, is incredibly popular and has made the state one of the most economically equal places in America. Importantly, Alaskans do not consider it "redistribution," but rather "joint ownership."[129]

Conclusion

While the guaranteed annual income pushes the envelope in terms of our shared sense of the mutual obligations we have to each other, it does not solve the puzzle of retirement security. Most plans assume that the GAI would stop where Social Security picked up. Neither the GAI nor Social Security depends on unearned income, but for government programs to adequately provide for our retirement, either our living costs must be reduced or more resources will need to be found. Fortunately, resources are available, as discussed in the next chapter.

CHAPTER 9

Where Will the Resources Come From?

Reflecting on the ideas for increasing income security, a question immediately rises: while they may all sound wonderful, how could we possibly afford to pay for them in an economic situation that has become so tight? How can we deal with these needs without further aggravating the reality that our economies are liquidating ecological capital and degrading Earth's bio-productivity?

We live in a "now" and "not yet" world. If we think outside the constraints of business as usual, and if we attend to promoting the common good rather than to enabling private gain, there are many possibilities in the "now" world for restoring lost revenue to the public sector and moderating the trajectory of the growth economy. The suggestions below include potential savings to government from changes in tax structures, spending priorities, and oversight of the financial sector; savings to consumers through restructuring of debt; and reining in the inflationary costs of health care.

Recapture the Wealth that the Financial Economy Is Siphoning off the Real Economy

In a gradual but steady shift since the 1980s, more and more financial wealth, what David Korten calls phantom wealth, has been acquired by borrowing to speculate in markets for new financial products rather than by investing in the productive economy. This is why the growth in the global money supply that results from borrowing has paralleled the growth of the financial economy.

This financial wealth has been increasingly concentrated in the hands of a few. Financial wealth accumulated in the financial markets does little to add real wealth to the real economy. Yet it enables those who possess it to lay claim to the goods and services of the real economy.

What can be done? It will be a challenge to mobilize the political will to enact change, especially because the financial interests are so deeply involved in the political process. Yet, there are remedies that are conceptually simple. Indeed, many of them involve recreating policies that had been in place in past decades.

Income taxes. Following an 1895 decision by the Supreme Court that declared income taxes unconstitutional, there was no federal income tax until the 16th Amendment was ratified in 1913.

During World War I there was a graduated tax of one percent, rising to six percent on incomes over $500,000, and a top marginal rate above 75 percent, though the effective tax paid by the very wealthy was about 15 percent.

In the 1920s the top marginal rate was lowered to about 25 prcent. The top marginal rate increased steadily during the 1930s and especially during World War II. In the 1950s, the top marginal federal tax rate for income over $250,000 remained 91 percent (*Figure 4*). This could only mean that the voting public at the time felt that $250,000 was an adequate ceiling for a quest for wealth, and that anything beyond that was clearly a surplus that could more appropriately be recaptured for public benefit.

President Kennedy initiated a reduction in the top marginal rate to 70 percent that continued through the 1970s. By the end of the Reagan tax cuts the rate had dropped to 28 percent, and it has since been restored only to 39 percent. While it could be plausibly argued that $250,000 doesn't go as far now as it did in the 1950s, we could still tax wealth much more aggressively now without abandoning any central national principle.

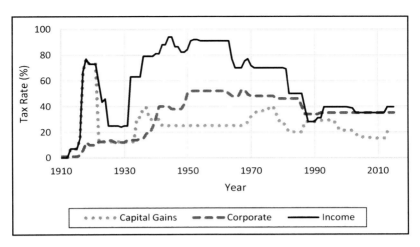

Figure 4. Top Marginal Tax Rates
Sources of data[130]

Capital gains taxes. Corporate and capital gains tax rates have been lower than income tax rates throughout most of the last hundred years (*Figure 4*). As of 2015, the U.S. federal government taxes long-term capital gains (assets held for over one year) at a rate of 15 percent for people who are in the 25 percent federal income tax bracket. There is no capital gains tax for the 10 percent and 15 percent income tax brackets, while a higher rate (20 percent) applies to those whose income exceeds $413,200 (singles) or $464,850 (married filing jointly).[131]

These capital gains tax rates are low by mid-twentieth century standards (*Figure 4*). State capital gains tax rates are zero in nine states and range from 7.4 to 13.3 percent in the 10 states with the highest rates.[132]

Low tax rates for capital gains are intended to stimulate investment. However, the resulting loss of tax revenue hampers public investment in infrastructure, public education, and other necessary public services. Considering the series of investment bubbles that have occurred over the past 20 years, public investment would be a better use of monies than speculative private-sector investments.

Corporate taxes. Corporate tax rates have likewise dropped (*Figure 4*). In 1960, 23 percent of total federal revenue came from corporate taxes. By 2013 this figure had shrunk to about 10 percent. This has come about in two ways: by lowering the corporate tax rate, and by creating a host of special deductions commonly known as "loopholes." In a parallel trend, the share of corporate income generated by production of goods and services declined, while the share generated by buy-outs and other financial transactions increased. So, as large corporations were providing fewer jobs while making more money on financial transactions, they were paying a lot less in taxes. It would be a conceptually simple matter — though politically fraught — to close corporate loopholes and bring that revenue back into the public sector.

Tax havens in foreign countries provide a major way for corporations, and wealthy individuals, to avoid paying taxes. At the end of 2011, 290 of the top Fortune 500 companies collectively held $1.6 trillion in profits outside the United States in tax havens — up from $1.1 trillion in 2009. This added up to $90 billion of lost federal revenue. With $90 billion from corporations and $60 billion from wealthy individuals, tax havens account for a total of $150 billion of lost federal tax revenues.[133] "Share the World's Resources" estimates that stopping these ways of avoiding taxes could bring in $349 billion in added taxes each year globally.[134]

Taxing financial transactions. The idea of a financial transaction tax (FTT), sometimes called a "Robin Hood tax," has been gaining momentum over recent years. The FFT is a very small tax applied to every sale and purchase of a stock, bond, or other financial instrument. It targets those who trade multiple times a millisecond, who are basically making money by using high speed computers to gamble on the financial market. For an investment that is held over a period of time, it would be a tiny percentage of its value. Several countries in Europe have been experimenting with such a tax, and legislation has been introduced in Congress to establish an FTT, projected to raise $1.2 trillion over the next decade.[135]

Taxing Fossil Fuels

End fossil fuel subsidies. Globally, the International Energy Agency estimates that the cost of government subsidies for fossil fuels increased from $311 billion in 2009 to $544 billion in 2012, the International Energy Agency estimates. Once lost tax revenues are included, this figure rises to around $2 trillion, equal to over 8 percent of global government revenues, according to a recent IMF report. As of July 2014, Oil Change International estimates U.S. fossil fuel subsidies at $37.5 billion annually, including $21 billion in production and exploration subsidies. With a pressing need to reduce fossil fuel use rather than expand it, that money should be used to meet other needs.[136]

A carbon tax with distributed dividends. According to climate scientist James Hansen, it is likely that a carbon cap-and-trade approach will become a tweak to business as usual. He and others argue that what is needed is a gradually rising fee on the carbon content of oil, gas, and coal, with proceeds distributed fully to the public. This will spur innovation in energy efficiency and carbon-free energy, while providing taxpayers with the funds needed to transition toward the clean energy world of the future. The economic reality is that we will not move to an era beyond fossil fuel emissions until a substantially higher price is applied across-the-board for all carbon fuels, such that efficiency and carbon-free energies rapidly increase. According to Hansen, the entire tax must be returned to the public, an equal amount to each adult, a half-share for children. This dividend can be deposited monthly in an individual's bank account. A carbon tax with a 100 percent dividend is non-regressive. By returning all the revenue, as equal share to each adult, a half-share for children, low and middle income people will find ways to limit their carbon tax and come out ahead. Profligate energy users will have to pay for their excesses.[137]

The Alaska Permanent Fund is a somewhat different form of this concept. More than 640,000 Alaskans currently receive annual dividends from Alaska oil royalties. Since it began in 1982, the Fund has paid out dividends ranging in amount from $330 in 1984 to over $2000 in 2008, for a total of

$22 billion. An Alaskan who has received every dividend will have collected more than $37,000.[138]

Reprioritize Federal Policies and Spending

Divert military spending. According to the Friends Committee on National Legislation, the core Pentagon budget grew by 50 percent in the last 12 years, and now is over $500 billion, not counting spending for wars in Iraq and Afghanistan. This is a level similar to the heights of Vietnam and Cold War spending. It dwarfs the military budgets of the next 29 biggest spenders in the world. Between $31 and $60 billion dollars were lost to waste and fraud related to the wars in Iraq and Afghanistan. Procurement and contract reform, better accounting methods and competitive bidding with military contractors could save billions of taxpayer dollars. Reducing the number of troops assigned to overseas bases by just 25 percent would save about $80 billion over the next ten years.[139]

For every 100 jobs created by Pentagon spending, the same investment would create 251 jobs in education, 169 jobs in health care, or 147 jobs in clean energy. For each federal tax dollar paid in 2013, the government spent about 40 cents on the military. Clearly, there is enormous potential for redirecting some of these resources toward meeting the basic needs of our people.[140]

Restore a commitment to government policies and programs for the common good: Many of the policies and programs that have been eliminated as a result of unrestrained free-market ideology and its orchestrated attack on the efficacy of government participation and regulation have contributed mightily to the economic insecurity that plagues so many people, especially those whose incomes are already precarious and live from paycheck to paycheck.

Rethink Healthcare

Ensuring that we will have the money to pay for our health care in old age is one of the driving forces behind savings for retirement. Why are the costs of U.S. healthcare so much more than elsewhere, and what can be done about it?

Remove profit-making middle men: The main group that plays a middle-man role, of course, is the health insurance industry. Private health insurance, once managed by home-grown, tax-exempt companies dedicated to fulfilling public service missions, has evolved into a multi-billion dollar, largely for-profit industry controlled by the world's biggest investment houses. They have used their considerable financial and political clout to make the most of recent changes in our nation's health care system. The requirement of the Affordable Care Act to have health insurance has expanded their market base enormously. Investment in public programs has become a major source of private revenue, with health insurance companies steadily moving in on Medicare and Medicaid markets by offering managed-care plans to patients enrolled in these public programs.

Getting unbiased and trustworthy profit margin figures is a challenge. The major health insurance industry trade group suggests that its profits are minimal, only about one penny per dollar. Yet one penny for every health care dollar adds up, leading to one estimate of $347 billion over 10 years ending in 2019.[141]

The industry itself claims very modest earnings, dropping from seven percent in 2005 to closer to three percent after 2009. But critical analysts, pointing to announcements of robust financial health that companies make to stockholders, suggested a seven to eight percent profit margin in 2011.[142]

The larger question remains: do we want a health insurance system that profits investors and financial speculators? Could we use those pennies in better service of our health?

Hospitals. Even hospitals that exist to provide direct health services have become problematic. Many hospitals that functioned in the past as community-based non-profits, have been turned into for-profit institutions. The extent to which competitive hospital advertising has proliferated is stunning.

The average compensation packets for independent hospital CEOs in 2011 was over half a million dollars (with for-profit CEOs making as much as $20 million). With hospitals

103

buying up many independent doctors' offices, the costs they charge for facility fees often rise dramatically for exactly the same services, since their fixed costs are higher.

In the competitive challenge of getting the most possible out of Medicare payments, hospitals are pushing the limits to bill at the Medicare codes that have higher reimbursements. This trend costs taxpayers billions in inflated charges.[143]

Pharmaceuticals. Another big profit-maker in the health care field is the pharmaceutical industry. The global pharmaceuticals market is worth US$ 300 billion a year, a figure expected to rise to US$ 400 billion within three years. The 10 largest drugs companies control over one-third of this market, several with sales of more than U.S. $10 billion a year and profit margins of up to 30 percent. Six are based in the United States and four in Europe.[144]

According to a 2014 BBC report, five pharmaceutical companies made a profit margin of 20 percent or more in 2013: Pfizer, Hoffmann-La Roche, AbbVie, GlaxoSmithKline, and Eli Lilly. Drug companies spend far more on marketing drugs — in some cases twice as much — than on developing them. Other unethical practices include paying for favorable published research, colluding with chemists to overcharge, mis-branding, and wrongly promoting drugs. With some drugs costing upwards of $100,000 for a full course, and with the cost of manufacturing just a tiny fraction of this, it is not hard to see why these companies are so profitable. [145]

The good news is that sales of generics, which accounted for 57 percent of all dispensed retail prescriptions in 2004, rose to 86 percent in 2013. The Generic Pharmaceutical Association calculated that generic products saved the U.S. health system nearly $1.5 trillion over the past 10 years.[146]

The Case for a Single Payer System
Everyone — from the Commonwealth Foundation to proponents of single payer systems — agrees that the U.S. spends much more per person and as a percentage of gross domestic product (GDP) than any other industrialized nation. In 2006, the U.S. *per capita* healthcare cost was $6,714,

compared to the $2,880 median among other industrialized nations participating in the Organization for Economic Cooperation and Development (OECD), after adjusting for cost of living. The U.S. spent almost 16 percent of its GDP on healthcare compared to between seven percent and eleven percent among other industrialized nations. The U.S. has the highest rate of deaths among people less than 75 years old that are from heart attacks, strokes, diabetes and bacterial infections; the U.S. has 96 such deaths per 100,000 people while France has 55 deaths.[147]

It seems clear that Western Europe's single-payer health system model helps to contain costs and avoid unnecessary testing and procedures. As the single payer, it is in the government's interest to provide incentives for preventing disease, thus saving money down the road. In contrast, the private fee-for-service model of the U.S. has the incentive of making money from managing a disease. A primary focus on preventing illness rather than on managing and treating illness makes total sense for a nation's overall healthcare strategy.

A single payer model takes advantage of bulk-purchase goods and supplies, while having more leverage over pharmaceutical profits, and wholly eliminates the need for a health insurance industry. As we are envisioning new possibilities, we may want to look beyond Europe. There is something to be learned from examples like the network of hospitals in Bangalore, India that have provided twice as many surgeries as the Cleveland Clinic at a fraction of the cost.[148]

Reimagine the role of health care in old age. This discussion of how to rationalize our health care system is of pressing interest as a way to gather public money to better support us in our final years. Yet the issues are not just financial. It will come as no surprise that nearly half of health care expenditures happen in our senior years, with that percentage heavily weighted toward those over 85. Indeed, a large proportion of health care costs associated with advancing age is incurred in the year or so before death.

One of the realities that is incompatible with our current technological healthcare model is that mortality is neither preventable nor an illness. Mortality is the ultimate insult to Western medicine. No matter how much money we put into cutting edge research, technology, drugs and machines, we cannot cure it.

We need more than better systems for delivering traditional health care services to the elderly. We need to rethink our relationship to dying, to find a better balance between not giving up on those of our elders who have the spirit to live more good years if they can get through a health crisis, and allowing others whose meaningful lives are drawing to a close to depart with dignity. Can our doctors shift their focus from keeping people alive to one of listening to what makes life meaningful, and routinely discussing end-of-life goals? How can we get our elders who are facing death out of the hospitals and into hospice? How can we support family members to help ease that transition for loved ones?

Restore the Regulation of Finance and Banking

Banks. The deregulation of the banks over the last several decades, culminating in the 1999 repeal of the Glass-Steagall Act, has had troubling consequences. Glass-Steagall was passed in the 1930s in response to the bank speculation that led to the 1929 crash and the Great Depression. It separated the functions of commercial and investment banks, so that the risk to depositors' money would be minimized.

The repeal of Glass-Steagall allowed commercial banks to invest in derivatives and hedge funds, and led to firms like Citigroup investing in credit default swaps, all leading up to the crash recession of 2008, and the taxpayers' bailout of these banks and investment houses. Regulating the banks more closely again would guard against similar losses and expensive bailouts in the future, keeping more of the country's wealth in the hands of its people.[149]

Payday lenders. A variety of other financial institutions that make money from personal debt could use stricter regulation, with a goal of keeping more resources in the hands of the general public. Payday lenders, for example, have turned millions of small loans, most for $500 or less, into a $30 billion-a-year industry. For much of the twentieth century, most states imposed interest rate caps of 24 to 42 percent on consumer loans. But Reagan-era deregulation opened the door to non-bank lenders and higher rates. After 2000 the payday industry grew quickly, helped by easy Wall Street credit. Payday lenders in some states can charge nearly 400 percent annualized interest (including fees) on two-week loans, which traps people in a cycle of debt. Consumer advocates suggest one solution: a federal cap on non-bank consumer interest rates.

Credit card industry. Credit card companies are perhaps less extortionate, but have a much greater impact on the economy. In the 1960s, when community banking was the backbone of the U.S. economy, only the most prudent bank customers with stellar payment histories "earned" access to credit cards. The credit card industry took off as a result of the deregulation that started in the late 1970s, with the loosening of banking rules and interest rate restrictions.

According to a Federal Reserve Bank report to Congress, by 2010 about 70 percent of families had one or more credit cards, and in 2013 there were 26 billion transactions involving almost $2.5 trillion dollars. Consumers carried an aggregate total of $862 billion in outstanding balances on their revolving accounts at the end of the year. Credit card earnings have been almost always higher than returns on other commercial bank activities, with interest rates since early 1998 fluctuating between 13 and 16 percent.[150]

Although the 2009 credit card reform law stopped many of the industry's most blatant abuses, many banks are finding ways around the law and launching new fees not specifically banned by the law — an indication of the challenges of regulation in this field.[151]

Student debt. Student debt has soared in recent years. Colleges take in about $26 billion in federal student loans and about $10 billion in Pell grants for low-income students. Federal student aid funding is the source of nearly 90 percent of revenue for some for-profit colleges. The average tuition in this sector is nearly twice that of comparable two-year and four-year public colleges. With only about 13 percent of students, for-profit colleges are responsible for nearly half of all student loan defaults. It is troubling that a whole new industry has grown up around student debt collection.[152]

Promoting Not-for-profit Alternatives that Keep Wealth in the Real Economy

Credit unions. Credit unions are nonprofit, cooperative financial institutions — "people's banks" — where members pool their savings to be borrowed and loaned among fellow members, and surplus income is returned to members in the form of dividends. Each member purchases one share to join, and has one vote in electing the board of directors, which has the authority to set loan limits and interest rates. While traditionally they have been formed by people with a common bond, i.e., of work or religion, today many credit unions simply require that you live or work in a certain geographic area to become a member. With expanded services in recent years, a credit union can often be a member's primary financial institution. Federally insured but exempt from federal taxation, they often have higher interest and lower loan rates than other banking institutions.

The roots of modern credit unions lie in mid-nineteenth century initiatives in Europe to provide credit to poor workers and farmers. Edward Filene, a progressive Boston merchant who had begun profit sharing with his employees, came across credit unions in a village in India in 1907. He then worked with others on the first state credit union act in the United States, a forerunner of the Federal Credit Union Act of 1934.

Today there are about 8000 credit unions in the country, with almost 90 million members and $679 billion on deposit. Credit unions have enormous potential to advance democracy and increase local control of financial resources.[153]

Public banking. In 1919, a populist farmers' movement in North Dakota swept the elections which led to the establishment of a state bank that loosened the hold of outside financial interests on the local population. Just as the state bank was opening its doors, the populists were swept out of office and conservatives were in charge of a bank they had fought against for two years. But being able to borrow — bank-to-bank — at a fraction of the interest rate that their government would have to pay a private bank made good, conservative fiscal sense. So the bank prospered, decade after decade, prudently investing the state's money in state infrastructure and state enterprises. In the spring of 2009, in the wake of the great recession, when the other 49 states were in the red and the Bakken oil boom had not yet hit, North Dakota reported a record budget surplus.[154]

The success of the State Bank of North Dakota raises a big question: why should governments, when they need money, have no choice but to borrow from private banks at high rates? Why, when they have money, must they just watch as those big banks take their wealth out of state to invest it who knows where in who knows what? A replication of this model in other states and municipalities could make affordable loans to small business and students; save taxpayers on critical infrastructure like bridges, public transit and schools; eliminate billions in bank fees and money management for cities and states; support a vibrant community banking sector; and help enable overall sustainable prosperity.

Radical Re-Envisioning of the Monetary System

All of the proposals suggested above are based on existing models, either in our nation's present, in its not-too-distant past, or in the practice of other Western countries. They could be advanced by simple legislative acts, although the financial interests that influence our political process make such a prospect difficult.

A bolder vision for recapturing wealth being siphoned off into speculative financial markets lies in restructuring our monetary system so the government doesn't have to borrow from private banks to spend. This vision is unconventional, but has a solid basis in economic analysis. Because the system we have now is the only one any of us in the U.S. has experienced, it is easy to believe that this system is the only possible one. This is not true. Many of the leading critics of our current system regard monetary reform as an essential feature of the "not yet" world, in which economic activity is not energized by a growth imperative, but guided by an ecological imperative.

In 2012, two International Monetary Fund economists reviewed a proposal to reform the banking system that had been made by leading economists during the Great Depression. Called "the Chicago Plan," it proposed separating the loan-making function, which would be managed by private banks, from the money-creation function, which would be managed by the federal government.

Lending was still to be a private banking function, but they would only lend the money deposited with them for long-term savings, rather than creating money as credit by what the economists call "deposit creation." The authors of the Chicago Plan envisioned better control of business cycle fluctuations, elimination of bank runs, reduction of public debt, and dramatic reduction of private debt. Money creation no longer would require simultaneous debt creation. The IMF economists determined that implementing such a plan in the present would yield all those same results.[155] The Canadian government operated with much success for over forty years using major features of the Chicago Plan (*Sidebar p. 111*).

If the government reclaims its authority to issue currency as envisioned by the Chicago Plan, it would not have to borrow money from the banking system, and pay interest to the speculative financial sector. It could simply spend new non-interest-bearing dollars into circulation, to be used for needed infrastructure projects or other public purposes. The money would enter the economy as payments to private contractors, their suppliers, and the workers they employ.

Creating Money
in the Public Interest

The Bank of Canada was established in 1935 as a private bank, but in 1938, recognizing that money should be created in the public interest, the government turned the Bank into a public institution. The Bank was harnessed to finance Canada's war effort, infrastructure projects including the Trans-Canada highway, the St. Lawrence Seaway, and hospitals and universities across the country. It was mandated to lend not only to the federal government but to provinces and municipalities.[156]

This public credit was used to fund social programs like the Old Age Security Act and programs to assist World War II veterans with vocational training and subsidized farm land. Repayment on loans simply went back into government coffers.

In 1974, however, under the influence of the pure free-market philosophy of the Bank for International Settlements in Switzerland, the government of Canada stopped borrowing from the bank of Canada, and started borrowing through private banks, which then kept the interest. Since 1974 the federal government has paid out over 1.5 trillion in interest to private banks that previously would have been available for public programs.

A current lawsuit seeks to "restore the use of the Bank of Canada to its original purpose [which] includes making interest-free loans to the municipal/provincial/federal governments for 'human capital' expenditures (education, health, other social services) and/or infrastructure expenditures."[157]

The lawsuit argues that not only may the Bank of Canada lend interest-free to the government, it is obliged to. Two courts have now refused to throw the case out, which means that the Bank has to justify why they haven't been giving interest-free loans to the government, why the minutes of the meetings in Switzerland are kept secret, why true figures on revenue are not coming in. So far, this possible breach has yet to be explained and justified.

This kind of monetary reform could redirect resources that are often just re-circulating within the financial sector to create more financial wealth for the wealthy. Knowing that these resources could be used for public purposes, it is much easier to think about an economic system that could provide for all its young, disabled, unemployed, and retired citizens. According to many critics of the growth economy, this kind of monetary reform would also be an essential feature of the "not yet" world.

The "not yet" world will have to be characterized by mutually enhancing relationships between economic activity and the ecosystems that the economy affects. In the "now" world, the money supply is managed for private gain, and tends to exploit both human communities and ecosystems without regard for their stability and well-being. In the "not yet" world, the money supply would be managed to facilitate economic activity that enhances the stability and well-being of both human communities and ecosystems.

Conclusion

The resources for all of us to live our elder years without fear of destitution are there. We just have to be bold in naming them, and clear about what our nation's priorities should be. As people of faith, we are particularly well-equipped to speak with clarity about the values that underlie the shifts that are necessary. In this chapter, we have reviewed policies and programs that past experience has shown to be feasible. Yet these do not address the need for an ecologically integrated economic system and culture. In the chapter that follows, we consider how income security can be provided for the elderly in a context of altered expectations and responsibilities that the "not yet" world will require.

Down to Earth with an Eye to the Future

The current monetary system is destroying democratic society. *The monetary and financial systems are now systematically moving wealth from the middle and working classes to corporate and political elites, from the poor to the wealthy, and from borrower to lender.[158] The for-profit, debt-money system requires governments to increasingly impoverish public services, and load un-repayable debt on taxpayers. With deregulation and corrupting financial innovations, the monetary system is now revealed as a tool of wealth accumulation for the already wealthy,[159] rather than a public service that enables the equitable development of all citizens and all communities within society.*

A collective reconsideration of what the monetary system is for arises from the question of what the economy is for. If general agreement can be reached that a good economy should provide equitable access to the means of life for all people, and preserve and enhance the resources on which human settlement and cultural life depend, then the way the monetary system works becomes a matter of critical importance.[160]

Most modern governments have allowed the operation of their national currency system to be controlled by for-profit financial corporations. But why should a sovereign government, which has the essential authority to create and regulate the national currency, default on this responsibility in favour of the private banking industry? Why should a national government have to borrow the national currency from private banks? Why should a government have to pay millions in interest on borrowed money? None of this is necessary; it is simply a historically determined convention. The monetary system could just as well be set up as a non-profit, public service institution that [e]nsures adequate circulation of legal tender to all citizens, and funds public interest expenditures on a debt-free basis.[161] Monetary system reform of this sort is an essential step in the change over to an ecologically integrated economy.

Keith Helmuth[162]

Chapter 10

Moving Forward, Faith into Action

Introduction

The unbridled pursuit of unearned income is playing a pernicious role in our financial system. It is driving the economic inequality that is tearing apart the fabric of our society, as it is driving the economic growth that is threatening the future of life on Earth. As those with the most money focus all their energy and power on acquiring even more, they are wielding that power to control decision making at every level in the public sphere, and threatening the heart of our democratic traditions. A shared vision of an economy that works for the common good is being replaced by the domination of an ethos of hyper-individualism, promoting private gain and rewarding greed.

We are all deeply entangled in this system that is moving steadily away from serving the common good. As consumers, we are pawns in the game. As debtors, we are oppressed by it. As investors, we prop it up. As citizens, we are losing our power to it.

The goal here is not to flagellate ourselves with guilt or to expend all our energy in the pursuit of individual purity, but to find our place in the web, name the truths that we see, take the steps that are available to us, and put our efforts toward wider community and structural efforts. Those of us who care about these issues need to look straight at the implications of the values and beliefs that sustain us, and try to withdraw our support from systems that run counter to those values and beliefs. As we work to liberate our minds from the diets of half-truths and outright lies that we are fed, from comforting ignorance and numbing assurances that the experts have everything under control, we may find grace as well as challenge. We will certainly be better grounded to act with as much integrity as we can within this tangled web.

As Consumers

As consumers who identify as people of faith, we have tended to limit our perspective to the purchases that we make. We try to be moderate in how much we consume. We take into consideration the impact of that consumption, the energy sources and supply chains, and make choices that minimize our collusion with human rights abuse and destruction of the environment. In this book, we suggest that there are choices to be made well beyond eco-friendly products, sweatshop apparel, fuel-efficient cars, and renewable energy. They extend to the institutions where we keep our money, the types of financial advice that we purchase, the investment funds that we select — all the ways that we use the resources we have toward the goal of securing our economic well-being.

As Debtors

As debtors, we may be faced with personal and individual issues of integrity — how to control mindless or excessive spending; how to delay gratification and take on the discipline of living within our means; how to stand up to social pressures to consume. We might strategize in our families and communities about ways to limit or help pay off personal debt. Support groups for debtors might be helpful. Families or faith communities might choose to take on the student or personal debt of their members at lower interest rates.

More important in the long run, however, will be a willingness to bring our conversation about debt into the public sphere, as a public issue. This will require overcoming the feelings of shame and personal failure that come with being in debt. But our personal debt is part of a larger story about the policies of credit card companies and pay-day lenders. Our housing debt fits into the larger picture of mortgages being bundled and sold for speculative profit. Our student debt is part of a larger story around the transformation of higher education finance. As we start talking about the systemic aspects of the debts we feel most closely, we may be able to see debt on a larger scale more clearly, and systemic solutions may start to come into clearer focus.

The debt of poor countries will fit into a picture of centuries of extraction and exploitation by the wealthy, industrialized nations. Our national debt will be part of the larger story of the speculative financial sector siphoning off the wealth of the real economy, with the government left to pick up the pieces. The idea of debt jubilee may gain increased resonance as a legitimate step in the process of transforming our economic system into one that again has a goal of serving the common good.

As Investors

The genesis of this book was a concern about our role as investors. If our future security is pinned on hopes that the financial markets will keep growing, how can we ask hard questions about the negative consequences of that growth? If our hard-earned assets are in banks and investment houses that have siphoned real wealth into speculative bubbles, how can we wish for their failure? How can we question the very premise of our current interest-based system that has us on a growth trajectory that is driving us beyond the carrying capacity of the planet?

If, however, we can imagine and take steps toward a vision of a new kind of security, the link between the growth of financial markets and our future wellbeing can be broken.

We can begin to withdraw our allegiance from that system, feel freer to name the truths of the injustice and destruction it breeds, and call without mental reservation for policies to end its continuous and dangerous drain on our common wealth.

Some of the policies that have been suggested are very modest. Who can argue against the fairness of a tiny tax on every purely financial transaction — on money being used to make more money? Many other widely discussed proposals for regulating this sector provide a return to the common sense regulations that were put in place after the Great Depression to prevent and protect us from such bubbles and crashes.

Our goal is a financial system that works to expedite the movement of resources between those who earn and those who contribute to building the real productive wealth of society — all without a built-in imperative of growth that our finite biosphere can no longer tolerate. Government may need to play a different role here, not just as spender and saver of last resort borrowing money at interest from private banks, but with the ability to create and inject money directly into the economy through public projects.

Those of us who care about the overall health of our economy, now and into the future, would do well to learn about these critical issues with enough understanding to be able to advocate persuasively for the ones that align with our faith values. As investors, we also have more immediate work to do. Chapter Seven laid out a variety of very practical alternatives to investing in speculative financial markets. It is ironic that some of the earliest faith-based screens for socially responsible investing screened out activity related to gambling, yet much of the activity in the financial markets now is gambling: making money by betting on how the value of commodities or currencies or bundles of mortgages will change — in the next ten seconds, the next ten days, or the next ten months.

Each of us with investments has the opportunity to shift to a position of greater integrity: from maximizing personal return, to screening out traditional vices, to adding screens for newly understood dangers such as fossil fuels, to moving away from any investments that involve financial speculation (gambling) and investing only in projects that we actively support. There is rich opportunity for discernment — as individuals and in our faith communities.

As Citizens

As citizens, our relationship to the current economic system presents a very different set of challenges, which can be seen as the mirror image of those we face in our roles as consumers, debtors, and investors. While problematic entanglements are growing in our roles as consumers, debtors and investors, as citizens we are becoming increasingly marginalized. Financial interests have been working over the past thirty years strategically and relentlessly to alter national and international rules and institutions in ways that benefit them at the expense of people, communities and the environment. As they buy up elected officials, orchestrate rulings that give money the rights of human beings in elections, and create trade agreements that give global corporations the right to overrule national regulations that protect the common good, our democracy is endangered as never before.

For many of the changes that are discussed in this book to work, we need a vigorous democratic process. Ultimately, attention to forces that limit our democratic rights, such as the Citizens United ruling that allows unlimited money in election campaigns, becomes foundational to other efforts for change.

Re-imagining Retirement

We do not have to wait for the advent of a more robust democracy, however, to get clear about the interaction of the forces that are at work here, and to apply our faith values to current entanglements that we face and relationships we would choose to have. Issues around retirement fall squarely into this process.

Much of the impetus for individual investing these days is generated by fears about old age security. Workplace pension plans, which used to play a significant role in providing that security — for stable blue collar union and white collar professional jobs alike — have given way to voluntary employee savings through 401(k) plans.

There are at least four negative consequences of this shift. Responsibility and risk for old-age security has shifted decisively to the individual, further weakening our sense of collective responsibility. Millions of people are transformed in the process into fervent boosters of anything that will push the markets up. At the same time, a smaller percentage of the population is coming to retirement age with adequate resources, and those with the capacity to face old age with confidence have been increasingly separated from the majority, whose safety net is our fraying Social Security system.

As we reach for a place of integrity, we need to think, not just about how our personal investments can be more in line with our faith values, but how a system of old age security can work for everyone. This involves the consideration in Chapter Eight of different ways a society can organize to support our common social security and the discussion in Chapter Nine of where the resources could come from to make that possible.

There are other changes that could support old age security. Options for a shorter work week would give people more time to provide support for elderly and vulnerable family members. Community planning that encouraged multigenerational households, easily accessible amenities and robust public transit would give elders more options around aging in place.

As we widen our frame of reference, we can see how our perspectives on old age are embedded in our larger cultural values. We are immersed in narratives about individualism, an ever-expanding frontier, the miracles of modern medicine, and the market as the premier locus for problem-solving. We are sorely in need of narratives that replace individual effort and reward in a technologically driven world in denial about physical limits with those of tending our community ecosystems in a finite world where life and death are interrelated and quality of relationship replaces the market as a driver of value. This would fit with the ecological imperative of a massive downsizing of our fossil-fuel and extraction-driven northern economies.

This new vision for retirement also calls for a new vision of old age. With technology and "progress" deifying the new, both things and people that are old can easily come to be seen as passé, and of less value than the new. So an important part of the puzzle is the reclamation of the value of old age.

What if we could see the value of our efforts become more distilled as we gain experience? Traditional societies named this wisdom and valued it highly. The world is in need of traditional wisdom now as never before. As we move on from our physical prime, it makes sense to get some relief from the most arduous tasks, but there's no reason to make a sharp break from work to play. Rather, we can think of a continuous shift in the ways we contribute to community and society. In our older years, we have the opportunity to model for others what a life of meaning looks like without paid work at the center, make ecologically and financially thoughtful choices as we transition, demonstrate to others what gives life meaning, and engage in efforts to transform society for future generations.

Old Age Security

Our family was privileged to meet a Ugandan refugee in the 1980s. We helped her with a project of starting a school back home when it was safe to return, and finally had the opportunity to visit her in Northern Uganda several years ago.

She lived in a compound of about twenty people, including her daughter-in-law, five or six grandchildren, and a group of young people she had adopted or taken in over the years, several of them now young adults. There was also an old auntie, some distant relative whose connection to the family was never made clear to us. She moved around the compound with difficulty and clearly was suffering from some kind of mental confusion as well, but she was treated kindly, as just another member of this extended family. There was not a lot of extra money, but she had a place to sleep and there were enough hands to see that she was washed and fed. Here was old age security at its most basic.

—*Pamela Haines*

What does this mean in practice, beyond reducing our dependence on unearned income in general, and income from financial speculation in particular? It might involve changing our lifestyles so that we need less, thus reducing both the amount we need to save for retirement and our ecological footprint at the same time. It might mean strengthening family ties and building up family and community structures that help care for the elderly. Neighborhood aging-in-place services like hospice, intergenerational supports, cooperative home health businesses are among initiatives to support.

Re-imagining Higher Education

As was mentioned in Chapter 5, our crisis in the cost of higher education cries out for change. An educational system where the basic credentials required for above-poverty-level work are beyond the financial reach of most young people and their families is a system without a future. Elements of needed change include some form of student loan-forgiveness or debt jubilee, removing the profit motive from education, institutional cost containment, and a mix of family and public financing that doesn't leave college graduates in virtual debt slavery.

It would be instructive to learn from the countries that have decided that college education is as much a public responsibility as K-12. Germany began adding tuition fees in 2006, but gave them up in 2014. Many other northern European countries — Norway, Finland, Denmark, France and Scotland — also offer publicly supported higher education. Greece, Turkey, Brazil and Argentina do as well, with Chile poised to join the list.

It is time to rethink our systemic reliance on higher education requirements in hiring. It is time to reconsider the various ways in which people acquire knowledge and experience, and hire on the basis of demonstrated ability, competence or potential. Perhaps it is also time to revisit the apprenticeship model of preparing for adulthood. This is an area on which individuals who are in the position of hiring could move without enormous systemic change.

Whoever we are, we can all help our children and grandchildren, and other young people around us, to acquire the basic life skills that will be needed in the generations to come. These include the ability to recognize wisdom, even in unlikely places; freedom from class-based assumptions about which knowledge and skills have value; construction and repair skills of all kinds; confidence in problem solving; ecological intelligence and skills around food production and preservation; emotional intelligence, including an ability to handle conflict and help groups move forward; ability to notice where new information would help a situation; confidence and skills to locate and learn new information; freedom from dependence on external markets; and capacity to be content with little and value home-grown entertainment.

Time spent helping the young people around us develop such a knowledge and skill base to prepare them for the world to come may be just as valuable, or even more so, than time spent working to cover the costs of higher education.

Moving Forward

Ultimately, of course, we won't be able to solve either the retirement or the higher education puzzle without taking on the larger economic system. This means acting as citizens in the public arena, advocating for changes that bend the system toward serving the common good. "Faith Ecology Economy Transformation," an interfaith effort hosted by the Maryknoll Center for Global Concerns in Washington D.C., provides some thoughtful policy guidance (*sidebar, p. 124*)

Conclusion

How can we hold the whole concept of unearned income up to the light, and look squarely at the role it has played throughout recorded history in widening the gap between the haves and the have nots? How can we get our minds around the possibility that humans have already extracted raw materials and emitted wastes at a rate that the planet cannot sustain; that we can no longer afford an economic system that requires unlimited growth?

We are not alone with these questions and concerns. There is a vibrant and growing school of economic thought that is grappling with these issues, and suggesting models that could work into the future. This discussion needs the support of ordinary people who are willing to wade into a debate that has previously been jealously guarded by those who claim the right to control it by virtue of their expertise — to unapologetically bring our faith values into the arena, and be as unimpressed by expert credentials as the innocent child who pointed out that the emperor had no clothes.

It is an opportunity to learn a dance that weaves greater integrity and meaning into our lives. There are all kinds of different steps. There are steps in gaining clarity and courage, in building our personal understanding and will to act. There are steps in personal finance. How can my liquid assets support community resilience? How can we be lenders and borrowers in a way that strengthens the social fabric of our communities rather than weakening it? How can my investing align most closely with my values?

There are steps in our families and communities. How can we reclaim some of the caring and security-building functions that have been monetized and taken over by large and distant profit-making institutions? There are steps in the larger arena. How can we join others in campaigns to call our institutions back to their vocations of serving the common good?

With many people dancing, we all can move from one step to another. For each of us, some of these steps will be easier to do than others. And at any one point in time, an individual may be doing only one step. But if we understand the dance, and see how each step is part of it, we can do the ones that are easy for us with joy, and teach them to others. We can stretch to try the harder ones, find those who have mastered them and stick close to learn what we can. We can value each step and each person who has joined in the dance. As we become stronger and more skilled, each small step of courage builds more solid ground under our feet. As we join others who are already doing the dance, and gather new ones in, we will be growing meaning and integrity in all our lives, as we play a role in reclaiming integrity in the public sphere.

Faith Economy Ecology Transformation
Draft Principles to Guide Economic and Environmental Policy Initiatives

We believe that humanity is being called to radically change its interactions with each other and Earth, and work together for changes at all levels of society to help build a new creation that is inclusive of all and that fits within the physical capacities of Earth. This will entail change from a focus on material goods to holistic well-being; from excess to sufficiency; from exclusion to inclusion; from competition to cooperation; from pursuing privilege to serving the common good; from the pre-eminence of humanity to the reverence for all life. Since specific economic and environmental policy initiatives are unlikely to address such broad goals, the following principles can help guide our response to such initiatives:

1. Global commons.

For the preservation of our future, the global commons must be protected. This includes not only our common air, oceans, fresh water, and biota, but our cultural heritage and accumulated information. In a system where material resources become more limited, this common wealth becomes increasingly precious and needs to be preserved for the common good and not subject to rules of private ownership.

Policy guidance:

Does it move toward the idea that basic resources are finite and a public good?

Does it tend toward a shift in the tax base, toward higher taxing of depletion and pollution?

Does it support the concept of putting the remaining commons into public trust?

Does it support the concept of the airwaves as a commons, with public regulation of media and advertising?

Does it support freeing knowledge from private ownership?

2. Wealth distribution and livelihood.

The goal of an economy is to ensure livelihood, not to make a profit. Resources and wealth should be distributed such that everyone can have a livelihood. Extreme wealth disparities damage both the wealthy and the poor.

Policy guidance:

Does it tend toward limiting the range of inequality and income distribution?

Does it tend toward a progressive consumption tax?

Does it strengthen a safety net to support subsistence for all?

Does it tend toward a living wage?

Does it tend toward flexibility in the length of working day/week/year?

Does it allow for greater regulation of capital mobility between countries, to better allow nations to prioritize meeting social needs?

Does it move away from "free trade," and encourage protection from standards-lowering competition from abroad?

3. Production.

Systems of production should be organized in a way that minimizes extraction, waste, and transport costs, and maximizes food access and durability of necessary goods. Systems of finance should be organized to support such production.

Policy guidance:

Does it encourage socially beneficial corporations?

Does it tax/regulate/subsidize in a way that minimizes extraction and waste?

Does it support alternative community-based financial institutions?

4. Governance.

Democracy requires that governments freely elected by the people, have the power to establish measures of common well-being and restrain institutions that are no longer serving the common good or are threatening the future viability of life on earth.

Policy guidance:

Does it support alternate ways of measuring societal well-being?

Does it limit fractional reserve banking?

Does it tend to limit control of the money supply by profit-making institutions?

Does it tend to limit the power of corporations?

Does it promote the concept of subsidiarity, of decision-making being located at the most local possible level?[163]

Endnotes

Full references are found in the Bibliography following.

1   The QIF Focus Books are listed on page ii. They are available from Keith Helmuth <keithhelmuth@gmail.com>, Quakerbooks <quakerbooks.org>. Amazon, and other online bookstores. See all the QIF Focus Books at <quakerinstitute.org>.

2   Adam Smith, 1776. (As discussed in Thomas R. Wells, 2014. Real-World Economics, No. 68, August 2014 <paecon.net/PAEReview/issue68/whole68.pdf>).

3   Franklin Roosevelt's Economic Bill of Rights, January 11, 1944<ushistory.org/documents/economic_bill_of_rights.htm> (accessed 15 December 2015).

4   David Graeber, 2011.

5   Aristotle, 350 B.C, Aristotle on usury <fauxcapitalist.com/2010/07/13/aristotle-on-usury> (accessed 17 December, 2015).

6   Biblical quotes use the New English Bible Version.

7   Stephen Zarienga, 2000.

8   Usury & Interest Rate in Quran <submission.org/usury_Interest_Rate.html> (accessed 15 December 2015).

9   Hencicliopedia, The Morals of Money-Lending <henciclopedia.org.uy/autores/Laguiadelmundo/Usury.htm> (accessed 15 December 2015).

10   New Advent Encyclopedia Usury <newadvent.org/cathen/15235c.htm>

11   Wayne Visser and Alastair McIntosh, 1998.

12   *Ibid.*

13   *Ibid.* and Bernstein, 1965.

14   Wayne Visser and Alastair McIntosh, 1998.

15   John Robertson, 2013.

16   Adam Smith, 1776.

17   John Maynard Keynes <maynardkeynes.org/> (accessed 15 December 2015).

18   Wayne Visser and Alastair McIntosh, 1998, and Julie Rehmeyer, 2010.

19   Matthew 6:14-30

20   William Herzog, 1989, pp. 150-168.

21   Omar Mason and Shahid M. K Ghauri, 2015.

22 John Woolman, 1763-4.

23 Chris Hedges, 2015. We are All Greeks Now *Truth Dig* July 15, 2015 <truthdig.com/report/item/we_are_all_greeks_now_20150712>. (accessed 15 December 2015).

24 Ellen Brown, Grexit or Jubilee <ellenbrown.com/2015/07/14/grexit-or-jubilee-how-greek-debt-could-be-annulled/>

25 David Howdon, 2013. Separating the Wheat from the Chaff: Icelandic and Irish Policy Responses to the Banking Crisis. *Economic Affairs*, October, 2013.

26 John Maynard Keynes <maynardkeynes.org/> (accessed 15 December 2015).

27 AFSC, 2004, reviewed by Keith Helmuth and Judy Lumb in *Quaker Eco-Bulletin* 5:2 <quakerearthcare.org/sites/quakerearthcare.org/files/qeb/qeb5-2-afscreport.pdf>.

28 Richard Wilkinson and Kate Pickett, 2009.

29 John Maynard Keynes <maynardkeynes.org/> (accessed 15 December 2015).

30 More detail on money, banking, and interest is found in QIF Focus Book #5, *It's the Economy, Friends* on pages 47-57, and also in #6, *Beyond the Growth Economy*, on pages 10-11.

31 Multiplier Effect (video) <investopedia.com/video/play/multipliereffect/#ixzz3oB86sgMP> (accessed 15 December 2015).

32 Kenneth Galbraith, 2001.

33 Henry Ford <brainyquote.com/quotes/quotes/h/henryford136294.html>

34 John Maynard Keynes <maynardkeynes.org/> (accesse1 15 December 2015).

35 Juliet Schor, 2015

36 Steve Frazer, 2015.

37 Michael Harrington, 1963

38 President John F. Kennedy, JFK on the Economy and Taxes <jfklibrary.org/JFK/JFK-in-History/JFK-on-the-Economy-and-Taxes. aspx>. (accessed 15 December 2015).

39 Crossing Wall Street, What's Good for General Motors Is God for America <crossingwallstreet.com/archives/2009/06/whats-good-forgeneral-motors-is-good-for-america.html> (accessed 15 December 2015).

40 David George, 2014.

41 Powell Memo <reclaimdemocracy.org/corporate_accountability/powell_memo_lewis.html>.

42 John Maynard Keynes <maynardkeynes.org/> (accessed 15 December 2015).

43 Joel Kurtzman, 1993.

44 Al Gore, 2013.

45 Oxfam, 2015 <oxfam.org/en/pressroom/pressreleases/2015-01-19/richest-1-will-own-more-all-rest-2016>.

46 Donella Meadows, et al,. 1972.

47 Herman Daly, 1973.

48 John Perkins, 2004

49 *Ibid.*

50 Inequality Video Fact Sheet <therules.org/inequality-video-factsheet> (accessed 15 December 2015).

51 Gro Harlem Brundtland, 1987.

52 Sustainable Seattle <sustainableseattle.org/about-us/visionmission> (accessed 15 December 2015).

53 Herman Daly and John Cobb, 1989, and many more.

54 Kenneth Boulding, 1965.

55 Charles Eisenstein, 2012. We Can't Grow Ourselves out of Debt, NO Matter What the Federal Reserve Does. *The Guardian* 3 September 2012. <theguardian.com/commentisfree/2012/sep/03/ debt-federal-reserve-f ixation-on-growth> (accessed 15 December 2015).

56 James Hansen quoted by Philip Shabecoff, "Global Warming Has Begun, Expert Tells Senate." *New York Times*, June 24, 1988.

57 Bill McKibben, 1989.

58 Ross Gelbspan, 1997. *The Heat is On*; Ross Gelbspan, 2004, *Boiling Point*; James Hoggan and Richard Littlemore, 2009, *Climate Cover-up: The Crusade against Global Warming*; Naomi Oreskes and Erik M. Conway, 2010, *Merchants of Doubt*: Robert Brulle, 2013, *Institutionalizing Delay: Foundation Funding and the Creation of U.S. Climate Change Counter-movement Organizations.*

59 Union of Concerned Scientists, 2015. *The Climate Deception Dossiers: Internal Fossil Fuel Industry Memos Reveal Decades of Corporate Disinformation* <ucsusa.org/sites/default/files/attach/2015/07/The-Climate-Deception-Dossiers.pdf> (accessed 15 December 2015).

60   Marina Fang, 2015. Jeb Bush: The Pope Shouldn't
     Discuss Climate Change because 'He's Not A Scientist.'
     Huffinton Post Octoer 1, 2015 <huffingtonpost.com/entry/
     jeb-bush-climate-change-pope_56047a10e4b08820d91c57bc>.

61   Sarah Westwood, 2015. Kerry says Paris agree-
     ment crafted to avoid Congress. *Washington Examiner*
     13 December 2015 <washingtonexaminer.com/kerry-
     says-paris-agreement-crafted-toavoid- congress/
     article/2578256>.

62   Ruth Roemer, Allyn Taylor, and Jean Lariviere, 2005. Origins of the
     Framework Convention on Tobacco Control. Amer. J. Public Health
     95(6): 936–938.

63   The Next System Project <nextsystemproject.org>

64   Lao Tse <brainyquote.com/quotes/quotes/l/laotzu121075.html>.

65   Joe Volk, 2011. Practicing Hope, Way Opens: Wilmington College
     Commencement Address <fcnl.org/about/who/staff/writings/
     practicing_hope_way_opens>.

66   Pope Francis, 2015. <vatican.va/content/francesco/en/
     speeches/2015/july/documents/papa-francesco_20150709_boliviamo-
     vimenti-popolari.html>.

67   Lisa Beyer, 2012. The Rise and Fall of Employer-Sponsored
     Pension Plans. *Workforce* <workforce.com/articles/
     the-rise-and-fall-of-employer-sponsored-pension-plans>.

68   Walser Wealth Management, Spring, 2015. Special Report: 401(k)
     ... America's Retirement Disaster. <walserwealth.com/wp-content/
     uploads/2015/05/SpecialReport401kSpring2015.pdf>.

69   Employee Benefit Research Institute, 2005. History of 401(k) Plans:
     An Update <ebri.org/pdf/publications/facts/0205fact.a.pdf>.

70   Lisa Beyer, 2012. The Rise and Fall of Employer-Sponsored
     Pension Plans. Workforce <workforce.com/articles/
     the-rise-and-fall-of-employer-sponsored-pension-plans>.

71   Scott Tong, 2013 Father of Modern 401(k) Says It Fails Many
     Americans. *Marketplace*. <marketplace.org/topics/sustainability/
     consumed/father-modern-401k-says-it-fails-many-americans>.

72   Geri Terzo, Demand Media. Effects of the Stock Market Crash
     <finance.zacks.com/effects-stock-market-crash-7707.html>.

73   Alice H Munnell. 401(k)/IRA Holdings in 2013: An Update
     from the Survey of Consumer Finance, Center for
     Retirement Research, September, 2014. <crr.bc.edu/briefs/
     401kira-holdings-in-2013-an-update-from-the-scf>.

74   Alicia H. Munnell, Anthony Webb, and Wenliang Hou. How Much Should People Save? *Center for Retirement Research* <crr.bc.edu/wp-content/uploads/2014/07/IB_14-111.pdf>.

75   Alice H Munnell. 401(k)/IRA Holdings in 2013: An Update from the Survey of Consumer Finance, *Center for Retirement Research*, September, 2014 <crr.bc.edu/briefs/401kira-holdings-in-2013-an-update-from-the-scf>.

76   Blaine Aikin and Nancy LeaMond, 2015. Enforce 'Conflict of Interest' Rule for Financial Advisers, Save Retirees. *Roll Call* September 9, 2015 <rollcall.com/news/enforce_conflict_of_interest_rule_for_ financial_advisers_save_retirees-243552-1.html?pg=1> (accessed 16 February 2016)

77   Michael Sivy. How Bad Is America's Pension Funding Problem? *Time Magazine* September 26, 2012 <business.time. com/2012/09/26/how-bad-is-americas-pension-funding-problem>.

78   Sheelalh Kolhatkar. Hedge Funds Are for Suckers. *Bloomberg Business*, July 11, 2013 <bloomberg.com/bw/articles/2013-07-11/why-hedge-funds-glory-days-may-be-gone-for-good> (accessed 18 December 2015).

79   Gregg S. Fisher. Chasing the Mirage of Hedge Fund Returns. *Forbes* January 23, 2012 <forbes.com/sites/greggfisher/2012/01/23/ chasing-the-mirage-of-hedge-fund-returns/> (accessed 18 December 2015).

80   Michael Sivy. How Bad Is America's Pension Funding Problem? *Time Magazine* September 26, 2012 <business.time. com/2012/09/26/how-bad-is-americas-pension-funding-problem> (accessed 18 December 2015).

81   Brice S. McKeever and Sarah L Perrijohn. The Nonprofit Sector in Brief 2014. *Urban* <urban.org/UploadedPDF/413277-Nonprofit-Sector-in-Brief-2014.pdf> (accessed 18 December 2015).

82   Kennard Wing, Katie Roeger, and Thomas H. Pollak. *Urban* September 14, 2010 <urban.org/uploadedpdf/412209-nonprofpublic-charities.pdf> (accessed 18 December 2015).

83   CF Insights. 2014 Columbus Survey Results: Sustained Growth in an Expanding Field <cfinsights.org/Knowledge/ViewArticle ArticleId/42/2014-Columbus-Survey-Results-Sustained-Growth-inan-Expanding-Field.aspx?_ga=1.81114263.1236301436.1450533377> (accessed 18 December 2015).

84   Center for Social Philanthropy and the Tellus Institute. Educational Endowments and the Financial Crisis: Social Costs And Systemic Risks in the Shadow Banking System <community-wealth.org/sites/clone.community-wealth.org/files/downloads/report-humphreys-et-al.pdf>. (accessed 16 February 2016).

85 Uebersax, John, 2009. College Tuition: Inflation or Hyperinflation? <wikipedia.org/wiki/College_tuition_in_the_United_States>.

86 U.S. Department of Education. *The Condition of Education 2012.* <nces.ed.gov/pubs2012/2012045.pdf> (accessed 18 December 2015).

87 Go Fossil Free, 350.org <gofossilfree.org>.

88 The Shalom Center, Move Our Money: *An Action Handbook* <theshalomcenter.org/content/move-our-money-action-handbook>.

89 Friends Fiduciary Corporation <friendsfiduciary.org> (accessed 18 December 2015).

90 Friends Fiduciary Corporation Green Fund <friendsfiduciary.org/quaker-green-fund/> (accessed 18 December 2015).

91 Quakers with a Concern for Palestine-Israel. Quakers Divest from Hewlett-Packard and Veolia Environment. End the Occupation, September 25, 2012. <endtheoccupation.org/article.php?id=3279> (accessed 10 February 2016).

92 John Fullerton, Capital Institute. *The Future of Finance: 6 Reasons Why Stock Markets Are No Longer Fit for Purpose.* <capitalinstitute.org/blog/6-reasons-why-stock-markets-are-no-longer-fit-purpose> (accessed 18 December 2015).

93 Keith Harrington, 2015.

94 Oblate International Pastoral Investment Trust <oiptrust.org/> (accessed 18 December 2015).

95 Patricia Kind Family Foundation <pkffoundation.net/> (accessed 18 December 2015).

96 Cutting Edge Capital <cuttingedgecapital.com> (accessed 18 December 2015).

97 President Barack Obama Signing JOBS Act, October 24, 2011. <whitehouse.gov/economy/jobsact> (accessed 18 December 2015) .

98 John Fullerton. Alternative Investment Methods. *P2P Foundation.* <p2pfoundation.net/Alternative_Investment_Methods> (accessed 18 December 2015).

99 Slow Money <slowmoney.org> (accessed 18 December 2015).

100 Mennonite Church USA Everence Agency <everence.com/who-weserve/> (accessed 18 December 2015).

101 Quaker Investment Ethical Trust <quaker.org.nz/qiet-quakerinvestment- ethical-trust> (accessed 18 December 2015).

102 World Council of Churches Oikocredit <oikocredit.coop>.

103 Kiva <kiva.org> (accessed 18 December 2015).

104 *The Economist*, March 1, 2014. <economist.com/news/finance-andeconomics/ 21597932-offering-both-borrowers-and-lenders-better-deal-websites-put-two> (accessed 18 December 2015).

105 Shelley Banjo, Wall Street is Hogging the Peer-to-peer Lending Market. Quartz, March 4, 2015. <qz.com/355848/wall-street-ishog-ging-the-peer-to-peer-lending-market/> (accessed 18 December 2015).

106 Amy Cortese. Loans That Avoid Banks? Maybe Not. *New York Times*, May 3, 2014. <nytimes.com/2014/05/04/business/loans-thatavoid-banks-maybe-not.html?_r=0> (accessed 18 December 2015).

107 Zopa P2P <zopa.com> (accessed 18 December 2015).

108 Social Welfare History Project <socialwelfarehistory.com/programs/ poor-laws> (accessed 19 December 2015).

109 David Beito, 2000. *From Mutual Aid to Welfare State: How Fraternal Societies Fought Poverty and Taught Character* <heritage.org/ research/lecture/from-mutual-aid-to-welfare-state> (accessed 18 December 2015).

110 Social Security *Historical Background and Development of Social Security* <ssa.gov/history/briefhistory3.html> (accessed 19 December 2015).

111 Huey Long's Share Our Wealth plan. <hueylong.com/programs/ share-our-wealth.php> (accessed 19 December 2015).

112 Franklin D. Roosevelt Day by Day <fdrlibrary.marist.edu/daybyday/ resource/june-1934> (accessed 19 December 2015).

113 Social Security Act of 1935 <ssa.gov/OP_Home/ssact/ssact-toc.htm> (accessed 19 December 2015).

114 Social Security History: Presidential Quotes <ssa.gov/history/ lbjstate. htm> (accessed 19 December 2015).

115 1972 Social Security Amendments <ssa.gov/history/1972amend. html> (accessed 19 December 2015).

116 Franklin D. Roosevelt State of the Union Message to Congress January 11, 1944. *The American Presidency Project* <presidency. ucsb.edu/ws/index.php?pid=16518> (accessed 19 December 2015).

117 Thomas Paine, 1795 *Agrarian Justice* <constitution.org/tp/agjustice. htm> (accessed 19 December 2015).

118 *Old Age in Colonial America* <ssa.gov/history/briefhistory3.html> (accessed 19 December 2015).

119 Jodie T. Allen. Negative Income Tax. *Library of Economics and Liberty* <econlib.org/library/Enc1/NegativeIncomeTax.html> (accessed 19 December 2015).

120 Mike Albert and Kevin C. Brown, Guaranteed Incomes's Moment in the Sun, *Remapping Debate* <remappingdebate.org/article/ guaranteed-income%E2%80%99s-moment-sun?nopaging> (accessed 19 December 2015).

121 Michael Harrington, 1963.

122 Martin Luther King, Jr., 1967 *Where Do We Go from Here: Chaos or Community?* <drmartinlutherkingjr.com/wherewearegoing.htm> (accessed 19 December 2015).

123 Richard Nixon. Address to the Nation on Domestic Programs, August 8, 1969. *The American Presidency Project* <presidency.ucsb.edu/ ws/?pid=2191> (accessed 19 December 2015).

124 Noah Gordon. The Conservative Case for a Guaranteed Basic Income. *The Atlantic*, August 6, 2014 <theatlantic.com/politics/ archive/2014/08 why-arent-reformicons-pushing-a-guaranteed-basicincome/ 375600> (accessed 19 December 2015).

125 Evelyn Forget, The Town with No Poverty. *University of Manitoba,* February, 2011 <public.econ.duke.edu/~erw/197/forget-cea%20 %282%29.pdf> (accessed 19 December 2015).

126 Truth-out. *What's Good About Guaranteed Basic Income.* July 3, 2015 <truth-out.org/opinion/item/31721-what-s-good-aboutguaranteed-basic-income> (accessed 19 December 2015).

127 Annie Lowrey. Switzerland's Proposal to Pay People for Being Alive. *New York Times* November 12, 2013 <nytimes.com/2013/11/17/ magazine/switzerlands-proposal-to-pay-people-for-being-alive. html?pagewanted=all&_r=0> (accessed 19 December 2015).

128 David R. Wheeler. What if the Government Guaranteed You and Income? *CNN*, April 14, 2014 <cnn.com/2014/04/14/opinion/wheeler-minimum-income> (accessed 19 December 2015).

129 Karl Widerquist. Alaska Dividend Blog. *Basic Income Guarantee* Network <usbig.net/alaskablog/about-the-alaska-dividend/> (accessed 19 December 2015).

130 Sources: Tax Policy Center <taxpolicycenter.org/taxfacts/displayafact. cfm?Docid=161; For Best Advice <forbestadvice.com/Money/Taxes/ Federal-Tax-Rates/Historical_Federal_Capital_Gains_Tax_Rates_ History.html>; and Tax Foundation <taxfoundation.org/article/ us-federal-individual-income-tax-rates-history-1913-2013-nominal-and-inflation-adjusted-brackets> (accessed 19 December 2015).

131 Bill Bischoff. Capital gains: At What Rate Will your Long-term Sales be Taxed? *Market Watch* February 23, 2015 <marketwatch.com/ story/capital-gains-at-what-rate-will-your-long-term-sales-betaxed- 2015-02-18> (accessed 19 December 2015).

132 Duggan, Wayne. Benzinga April 1, 2015 <benzinga.com/general/ education/15/04/5357700/these-10-states-have-the-highest-capitalgains- taxes> (accessed 19 December 2015).

133 United States Public Interest Research Group Education Fund, January 2013 <uspirgedfund.org/sites/pirg/files/reports/USPIRG_ State_Tax_Havens.pdf> (accessed 19 December 2015).

134 Share the World's Resources <sharing.org> (accessed 19 December 2015).

135 McElwee, Sean, and Lenore Palladino. Smart Way to Stop Wall Street's Reckless Behaviour. *New Republic*, January 12, 2015 <newrepublic.com/article/120755/chris-van-hollen-financialtrans- action- tax-would-curb-risky-trading> (accessed 19 December 2015).

136 Oil Change International *Fossil Fuel Subsidies*: Overview <priceofoil. org/fossil-fuel-subsidies> (accessed 19 December 2015).

137 Hansen, James, 2009. Can We Reverse Global Climate Change? *Global Policy Forum*, May 14, 2009. <globalpolicy.org/social- andeconomic- policy/global-taxes-1-79/energy-taxes/47845.html> (accessed 19 December 2015).

138 1,884: The amount of the 2014 Alaska Permanent Fund dividend. *Daily News-Miner*, September 17, 2014. <newsminer.com/news/ local_news/the-amount-of-the-alaska-permanent-fund-dividend/ article_2a815156-3e92-11e4-966a-0017a43b2370.html> (accessed 19 December 2015).

139 Jim Cason *Friends Committee on National Legislation* March 2014 <fcnl.org/assets/pubs/March_2014_Jims_Letter.pdf> (accessed 19 December 2015).

140 Friends Committee on National Legislation. *Protecting Jobs through Responsible Reductions*. November 2012 <fcnl.org/pdfs/issues/ budget/Jobs_vs_Military_Final.pdf> (accessed 19 December 2015).

141 Ethan Rome. The Turth about Health Insurance Companies Profits: They're Excessive. *Huffington Post* May 18, 2011. <huffingtonpost. com/ethan-rome/the-truth-about-health-in_b_863632.html>.

142 Chris Conover. Profits in Health Insurance under Obamacare *Forbes*, June 27, 2014 <forbes.com/sites/theapothecary/2014/06/27/ profits-in-health-insurance-under-obamacare/#b6824ec4c42a>.

143 Fred Schulte and David Donald, How Doctors and Hospitals Have Collected Billions in Questionable Medicare Fees. *The Center for Public Integrity*, September 15, 2012 <publicintegrity. org/2012/09/15/10810/how-doctors-and-hospitals-have-collectedbil-lions- questionable-medicare-fees> (accessed 19 December 2015).

144 Trade, Foreign Policy, Diplomacy and Health: Pharmaceutical Industry. *World Health Organization*, 2015 <who.int/trade/glossary/ story073/en> (accessed 19 December 2015).

145 Richard Anderson, Pharmaceutical Industry Gets High on Fat Profits. *BBC News*, November 6, 2014 <bbc.com/news/ business-28212223>.

146 Generic Pharmaceutical Association, Generic Drug Savings in the U.S. *IMS Institute for Healthcare Informatics* <gphaonline.org/media/ cms/GPhA_Generic_Cost_Savings_2014_IMS_presentation.pdf> (accessed 19 December 2015).

147 David Squires *Commonwealth Foundation* July 18, 2012 <epianaly-sis.wordpress.com/2012/07/18/usversuseurope> (accessed 19 December 2015).

148 Susan Scutti. Why Emerging Economies Should Ignore Western Health Care Models <ncbi.nlm.nih.gov/pmc/articles/PMC1361028> (accessed 19 December 2015).

149 Wallace Turveville. Owning of the Consequences: Clinton and the Repeal of Glass-Steagall, *Policyshop* <demos.org/blog/9/11/15/ owning-consequences-clinton-and-repeal-glass-steagall> (accessed 19 December 2015).

150 Federal Reserve Report to Congress, June 2014 <federalreserve. gov/publications/other-reports/files/ccprofit2014.pdf> (accessed 19 December 2015).

151 A Short History of Financial Deregulation in the United States <open-thegovernment.org/sites/default/files/otg/deregtimeline- 2009-07.pdf> (accessed 19 December 2015).

152 Chris Kirkham. For-profit Colleges that Bury Students in Debt Face Second Obama Crackdown, *Huffinton Post* March 13, 2014 <huffing-tonpost.com/2014/03/13/for-profit-collegesobama_ n_4961163.html> (accessed 19 December 2015).

153 Randolph-Brooks Federal Credit Union. *History of Credit Unions*. <rbfcu.org/NB/html/Reference/AboutUs/RBFCUHistory.htm> (accessed 19 December 2015).

154 Joel Harkinson. How the Nation's Only State-Owned Bank Became the Envy of Wall Street. *Mother Jones* March 27, 2009 <motherjones. com/mojo/2009/03/how-nation%E2%80%99s-onlystate-owned-bank-became-envy-wall-street> (accessed 19 December 2015).

155 Jaromir Benes and Michael Kumhof. The Chicago Plan Revisited. *International Monetary Fund*, 2012 <imf.org/external/pubs/ft/ wp/2012/ wp12202.pdf> (accessed 19 December 2015).

156 Bank of Canada. *The Bank's History* <bankofcanada.ca/about/ history> (accessed 19 December 2015).

157 Global Research News. *The Case to "Reinstate" the Bank of Canada*, February 7, 2015. <globalresearch.ca/the-case-to-reinstatethe- bank-of-canada/5430132> (accessed 19 December 2015).

158 David Korten, 2010.

159 Charles Ferguson, 2012.

160 Francis Hutchinson, Mary Mellor, and Wendy Olson, 2002.

161 Joseph Huber and James Robertson, 2010; James Robertson, 2012; and Bollier and Conaty, 2015.

162 Keith Helmuth, 2015.

163 Faith Ecology Economy Transformation <faitheconomyecology.word-press.com>.

Bibliography

350.org. Go Fossil Free. <gofossilfree.org> (accessed July 2, 2015)

American Friends Service Committee (AFSC), 2004. *Putting Dignity & Rights at the Heart of the Global Economy* <afsc.org/sites/afsc.civicactions.net/files/documents/58202.pdf> (accessed 18 December, 2015)

Bernstein, J. L., 1965. "The Checkered Career of Usury," in American Bar Association Journal 51: 846.

Bollier, David, and Pat Conaty, 2015. *Democratic Money and Capital for the Commons: Strategies for Transforming Neoliberal Finance Through Commons-Based Alternatives.* Berlin, Germany: Commons Strategies Group Workshop with Heinrich Böll Foundation <bollier.org/democratic-money-and-capital-commons-report-pdf>.

Boulding, Kenneth E., 1965. *Earth as a Spaceship, an Essay for the Committee on Space Sciences*, Washington State University. 10 May 1965. Archives (Box #38) Colorado State University <colorado. edu/econ/Kenneth.Boulding/ spaceship-earth.html>.

Brown, Peter G., Geoffrey Garver with Keith Helmuth, Robert Howell, and Steve Szeghi, 2009. *Right Relationship: Building a Whole Earth Economy.* San Francisco CA: Berrett-Kohler.

Brundtland, Gro Harlem, 1987. *Report of the World Commission on Environment and Development: Our Common Future.* United Nations Environment Programme <un-documents.net/our-common-future.pdf>.

Daly, Herman, ed. 1973. *Toward a Steady-state Economy.* London: W.H. Freeman.

Daly, Herman, and John Cobb Jr., 1989. *For The Common Good: Redirecting the Economy Toward Community, the Environment, and a Sustainable Future.* Boston MA: Beacon Press.

Ferguson, Charles, 2012. *Predator Nation: Corporate Criminals, Political Corruption, and the Hijacking of America.* New York NY: Random House.

Frazer, Steve. 2015. *The Age of Acquiescence: The Life and Death of American Resistance to Organized Wealth and Power.* Boston MA: Little, Brown, and Company.

Fullerton, John, Capital Institute <capitalinstitute.org> (accessed November 9, 2015).

Galbraith, John Kenneth, 2001. *Money: Whence It Came, Where It Went.* Boston MA: Houghton Miffin.

George, David, 2014. *The Rhetoric of the Right: Language Change and the Spread of the Market.* London UK: Routledge Press.

Gore, Al, 2013. *The Future: Six Drivers of Global Change.* New York NY: Random House.

Graeber, David, 2011. *Debt: The First 5000 Years.* New York NY: Melville House Books.

Harrington, Keith, 2015. Why Slower Money Is the Key to a Real Economic Recovery. *Yes Magazine* October 22, 2015 <yesmagazine.org/new-economy/patient-finance-why-slower-money-is-thekey-to-a-real-economic-recovery> (accessed November 9, 2015).

Harrington, Michael, 1963. *The Other America: Poverty in the United States.* New York NY: Simon & Schuster, Inc., First Touchstone Edition 1997.

Helmuth, Keith, 2015. *Tracking Down Ecological Guidance: Presence, Beauty, Survival.* Woodstock, NB: Chapel Street Editions.

Herzog, William R., II, 1994. *Parables as Subversive Speech: Jesus as Pedagogue of the Oppressed.* Louisville KY: Westminster John Knox Press.

Huber, Joseph and James Robertson, 2010. *Creating New Money: A Monetary Reform for the Information Age.* London UK: New Economics Foundation. <neweconomics.org.uk>.

Hutchinson, Francis, Mary Mellor, and Wendy Olson, 2002. *The Politics of Money: Towards Sustainability and Economic Democracy.* London UK: Pluto Press.

Korten, David C., 2010. *Agenda for a New Economy: From Phantom Wealth to Real Wealth,* 2nd Edition. San Francisco CA: Berrett-Koehler

Kurtzman, Joel, 1993. *The Death of Money: How the Electronic Economy Has Destablized the World's Markets and Created Financial Chaos.* Boston MA: Little Brown.

Mason, Omar and Shahid M. K. Ghauri, 2015. *The Rightful Way of Banking.* Cambridge UK: Cambridge Scholars.

Meadows, Donella, Dennis Meadows, Jorgen Randers and William Behrens, III, 1972. T*he Limits to Growth: A Report for the Club of Rome's Project on the Predicament of Mankind.* New York NY: Universe Books.

McKibben, Bill, 1989. *The End of Nature.* New York: Anchor. Perkins, John, 2004. Confessions of an Economic Hit Man. San Francisco, CA: Berret-Koehler Publishers, Inc.

Perkins, John, 2004. *Confessions of an Economic Hit Man.* San Francisco, CA: Berret-Koehler Publishers, Inc.

Rehmeyer, Julie, 2010. 'Discounting' the Future Cost of Climate Change. *ScienceNews* <sciencenews.org/article/

discounting-future-cost-climate-change> (accesssed 15 December 2015).

Robertson, James, 2012. *Future Money: Breakdown or Breakthrough.* Totnes, Devon UK: Green Books.

Robertson, John M., ed. 2013. *The Philosophical Works of Francis Bacon,* first published in 1905, based on seven volume edition of 1857.

Schor, Juliet, 2015. *Juliet Schor Keynote* <trinitywallstreet.org/video/juliet-schor-keynote> (accessed November 9, 2015).

Sherman, Matthew. 2009. *A Short History of Financial Deregulation in the United States.* Washington D.C.: Center for Economic and Policy Research. <openthegovernment.org/sites/default/files/otg/dereg-timeline-2009-07.pdf> (accessed July 23, 2015).

Smith, Adam, 1776. *The Wealth of Nations.* New York: Random House, Inc. 1937 <marxists.org/reference/archive/smith-adam/works/wealth-of-nations>.

Stern, Nicholas. 2006. *The Economics of Climate Change: The Stern Review.*

Visser, Wayne A. M. and Alastair McIntosh, 1998. A Short Review of the Historical Critique of Usury. *Accounting, Business and Financial History* 8:2. <alastairmcintosh.com/Articles/1998_usury.htm> (accessed July 2, 2015).

Waskow, Rabbi Arthur, 2014. *Move Our Money: An Action Handbook.* <theshalomcenter.org/content/move-our-money-action-handbook> (accessed July 2, 2015).

Wilkinson, Richard and Kate Pickett, 2009. *The Spirit Level: Why Greater Equality Makes Societies Stronger.* New York NY: Bloomsbury Press.

Woolman, John 1763-4. *Plea for the Poor or a Word of Remembrance and Caution to the Rich.* <umilta.net/woolmanplea.html> (accessed 15 December 2015).

Zarienga, Stephen, 2000. A Brief History of Interest. *American Monetary Institute, Research & Articles,* December 28, 2010. <monetary.org/a-brief-history-of-interest/2010/12> (accessed 17 December, 2015).

Quaker Institute for the Future

Advancing a global future of inclusion, social justice, and ecological integrity through participatory research and discernment.

The Quaker Institute for the Future (QIF) seeks to generate systematic insight, knowledge, and wisdom that can inform public policy and enable us to treat all humans, all communities of life, and the whole Earth as manifestations of the Divine. QIF creates the opportunity for Quaker scholars and practitioners to apply the social and ecological intelligence of their disciplines within the context of Friends' testimonies and the Quaker traditions of truth seeking and public service.

The focus of the Institute's concerns include:

- Moving from economic policies and practices that undermine Earth's capacity to support life to an ecologically based economy that works for the security, vitality and resilience of human communities and the well-being of the entire commonwealth of planetary life.

- Bringing the governance of the common good into the regulation of technologies that holds us responsible for the future well-being of humanity and the Earth.

- Reducing structural violence arising from economic privilege, social exclusion, and environmental degradation through the expansion of equitable sharing, inclusion, justice, and ecosystem restoration.

- Reversing the growing segregation of people into enclaves of privilege and deprivation through public policies and public trust institutions that facilitate equity of access to the means life.

- Engaging the complexity of global interdependence and its demands on governance systems, institutional accountability, and citizen's responsibilities.

- Moving from societal norms of aggressive individualism, winner-take-all competition, and economic aggrandizement to the practices of cooperation, collaboration, commonwealth sharing, and an economy keyed to strengthening the common good.

CPSIA information can be obtained at www.ICGtesting.com
Printed in the USA
BVOW02s0141230416

445044BV00003B/5/P